Praise for Christopher Paul Jones

'Jones specialises in helping people let go of their fears, anxieties and phobias. From fear of public speaking to anxieties around work, Jones has helped hundreds of people get their lives back.'
– GQ

'I have never liked flying much, but after an especially bumpy journey last year I booked myself to have a two-hour session with celebrated fear coach Christopher Paul Jones, the Breakthrough Expert ... [On my next journey] I felt an unusual sense of calm going through customs, took my seat quite happily and chatted with my friends as the flight took off (which I didn't give a second thought about).'
– Hello!

'What Chris does is scramble the brain's thoughts [and] doing so he creates new, healthy patterns of thinking that stop anxious thoughts from taking over ... As we move through the exercises, Chris asks me to rate my fear on a scale of 1 to 10. Each time I revisit to the scenario, the fear surprisingly becomes less palpable. On the way home, I take the Tube, and my fear has significantly lessened.'
– Evening Standard

'With his method, Christopher helped me pinpoint where my phobia was coming from and gave me tools to help reduce my anxiety levels.'
– PopSugar

'If you find that your phobia is preventing you from living life to the fullest, I'd highly recommend visiting Christopher to regain your freedom!'
– Yours magazine

'Travelling home after our consultation I felt notably relaxed and calm. Christopher has given me a whole range of techniques to use if I feel myself getting anxious again and I now feel a lot more confident and prepared to deal with life's challenges.'
– Your Healthy Living

FACE YOUR FEARS

7 Steps to Conquering Phobias and Anxiety

Christopher Paul Jones

Michael O'Mara Books Limited

First published in Great Britain in 2024 by
Michael O'Mara Books Limited
9 Lion Yard
Tremadoc Road
London SW4 7NQ

Copyright © Christopher Paul Jones 2024

Client names and identifying details have been changed to protect the privacy of individuals whose stories are told herein. Although the author has made every effort to ensure that the information in this book was correct at the time of publication, the author does not assume any liability to any party for any loss, damage or disruption caused by errors or omissions. This book is not intended as a substitute for professional advice and support.

A CIP catalogue record for this book is available from the British Library.

This product is made of material from well-managed, FSC®-certified forests and other controlled sources. The manufacturing processes conform to the environmental regulations of the country of origin.

ISBN: 978-1-78929-532-0 in paperback print format
ISBN: 978-1-78929-533-7 in ebook format

1 2 3 4 5 6 7 8 9 10

Cover design by Natasha Le Coultre
Cover images by Shutterstock
Designed and typeset by Claire Cater
Printed and bound by CPI Group (UK) Ltd, Croydon, CR0 4YY

www.mombooks.com

MIX
Paper | Supporting
responsible forestry
FSC® C171272
FSC
www.fsc.org

CONTENTS

ACKNOWLEDGEMENTS

Firstly, I would like to say a big thank you to my family and friends. Your patience and understanding, feedback, constructive criticism and insightful discussions have played a vital role in shaping my words.

I would also like to extend my gratitude to the many colleagues, teachers, mentors, thinkers and researchers whose work has contributed to my ideas over the years. Your dedication to your respective fields has inspired me.

To my editor and publishing team, thank you for your expertise, dedication and belief in this project.

And last but by no means least, I want to express my heartfelt appreciation to you, the reader. I sincerely hope that what you read in these pages resonates with you and inspires you to make a positive change for yourself and others.

INTRODUCTION: FACE YOUR FEAR

Being gripped by a fear or phobia can massively affect your life. The adrenaline rush at the sight of that thing you fear, the gut-wrenching feeling that makes your heart pound and your palms sweat, can feel debilitating.

It was like this for me for a significant part of my life.

I suffered from several phobias. I had a list: flying, public speaking and bugs were just the tip of the iceberg. A traumatic experience with a helicopter had me avoiding flying at any cost, and the laughter of my classmates still echoed in my mind any time I was asked to speak, after being forced to get up and read in front of a class when I was young.

My phobias limited my choices, drained away my joy and stopped me from having the freedom I craved. One day, I realized I needed to take control, or I would always be a victim of my fears.

I embarked on a journey to find the most effective ways to change. I became a passionate student of the human psyche. I learned many forms of therapy and change work – cognitive behavioural therapy (CBT), clinical hypnotherapy, neuro-linguistic programming (NLP), eye movement desensitization and reprocessing (EMDR), psychotherapy and mindfulness, among others.

The result? Well, I was able to let go of my fears. It's hard to describe just how amazing it felt to fly and see the world or talk on stage without nerves or worry. Additionally, my life was more peaceful as I was no longer living with the constant anticipation of threat or danger.

Resolving my own issues started me on the path to becoming a therapist and coach. I knew I could do for others what I had done for myself, so I took what I'd learned, reflected on my personal experience of what worked and what didn't and collated what I felt were the best, most effective ways to change a phobia.

This became the foundation for my rapid change method, the Integrated Change System™ (ICS).

Today, I am considered one of the UK's leading experts on phobias. I have been featured on TV shows and in magazines, and I count movie stars and celebrities among my clients. Many, many terrified people have walked through my doors, and they leave entirely free from fear, sometimes in just one short session. I hope that with this book I'll be able to help you tackle your phobia too.

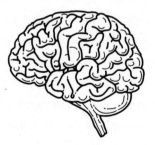

WHY WRITE THIS BOOK?

When I wrote this book, the world was still recovering from the effects of the COVID-19 pandemic. As lockdowns ended and people seemingly returned to normal, I noticed one thing: fears, phobias and anxiety seemed to have almost become a new pandemic themselves.

People began contacting me, saying that previously mild fears had transformed into crippling phobias. Simple activities they hadn't done in a while, like travelling or meeting people in groups, had suddenly become overwhelming. Some had developed severe germ phobias, moderate issues had become extreme, and mild stress had transformed into acute anxiety.

I knew my experience and methods could be used to help change this downward trend, and while my one-to-one sessions and trainings could help many people, the fastest way to help the greatest number of people was to put pen to paper and write this book.

What you hold in your hands is a roadmap to overcoming your phobias. *Face Your Fears* is a different and original approach to tackling what you are afraid of. In this step-by-step guide, we will look at the science behind fears and phobias: why our mind creates them, what's happening in our brains and bodies when we are triggered and what can be done to change it.

We will look at the most up-to-date and effective practical tools, tips and techniques for overcoming your phobia, and we'll review the seven steps in the ICS and look at how to use them. This will likely be different from other methods you may have tried, as it's not just about telling yourself not to be scared or trying to expose yourself to the thing you are fearful of. Instead, you will be changing how your mind and body process the response, thus helping you remove it.

We will explore the most well-known phobias, examine their

myths and realities, and look at how common each of them are. We will also look at examples of clients and celebrities who have had these fears and how they overcame them.

As I write this introduction, I'm reflecting on my journey from growing up in a small English village to working with many different types of people from all walks of life and from all over the world. Over the years, I have worked with everyone from accountants to artists, boxers to businessmen. I've helped dancers, musicians, Oscar nominees, people in the police force, military and government, and even royalty!

What I have found is that regardless of age, religion, culture, politics, identity, physical strength, intellect, gender or life perspectives, we are not all that different, and we can all develop irrational phobias, often rooted in the most unexpected, seemingly strange things.

When people ask why I do what I do, I tell them it's not only about helping others let go of fears and phobias; it's about helping them get their freedom back to live life to the fullest – on their terms. My wish is that this book will do the same for you.

I have seen how phobias can stop people from living their best lives and the world of possibilities that opens up to them when they free themselves from whatever is holding them back. By the time you reach the end of this book, you will have the information, tools and confidence you need to let go of your fears, however deep-rooted they are and however overwhelming they may seem.

HOW TO USE THIS BOOK

I've divided this book into three major sections, and studying these areas will enable you to explore, examine and eradicate your fears.

First, we will look at how phobias start, the science behind them, what's happening in the brain and the cognitive distortions our mind makes when we are fearful.

Next, we'll explore the best tools and latest methods for overcoming phobias. Here, you'll learn about the ICS and my seven steps for transforming a phobia.

Finally, we'll look at the top ten most common phobias. We'll review case studies, debunk the myths and uncover the truth about these fears. This will help you challenge those old limiting thoughts.

I recommend you read this book in order; however, if you need a solution quickly, you can skip straight to Part 2 or use the quick recap at the end of each chapter.

Additionally, as a thank-you for buying this book I'm also gifting you some bonus content. Scan the QR code below and you'll be able to access video introductions to each chapter and other resources to help you face your fear.

Are you ready to begin? Great!

Let's start by looking at the science of your phobia.

PART 1

How Phobias Are Created

WHERE DO OUR PHOBIAS COME FROM?

A few years ago, I had the opportunity to work with a client who had served in the military. He was rather secretive about the details of his service and would not disclose which branch he was in. After some time trying to get this information out of him, I playfully asked, 'Are you part of the Special Forces or something?'

His expression remained unchanged and he replied, 'I can't tell you.'

Believing we were sharing a light-hearted joke, I responded, 'You mean you could tell me, but you'd have to kill me?'

To my surprise, he didn't laugh or even crack a smile. Instead, he solemnly repeated, 'I can't tell you.' Sensing that I had pushed the topic far enough, I swiftly moved on from that line of questioning.

As our conversation progressed, he opened up about a harrowing experience during his service. He recalled a time when he and his team were under enemy fire, desperately trying to reach the safety of a helicopter. 'I was terrified,' he admitted.

Thinking I was understanding his fear, I empathized: 'That's not surprising or irrational; anyone would be terrified of being shot at.' He looked at me with disbelief. 'I wasn't scared of being shot. I'm trained to deal with that. It was the idea of getting into the helicopter that terrified me.'

It was a striking revelation: this soldier, who faced gunfire and other dangers without flinching, was more afraid of boarding a helicopter that would carry him to safety than he was of being shot at.

Throughout my career, I've encountered numerous cases of people who put themselves in real danger to avoid the object or situation that triggers their phobia. For example, someone with a profound fear of insects might suddenly veer their vehicle into oncoming traffic, all because they spotted a tiny bug on their seat. In a bid to avert a perceived threat, they inadvertently create genuine peril.

The key takeaway from these experiences is that phobias are not logical, and simply telling someone not to worry or just to go ahead and face their fears without solid tactics usually has little to no effect. Their phobia has little to do with the actual likelihood of danger and is not a reflection of a person's intelligence or strength.

THE NEUROSCIENCE OF FEAR

As you dive deeper into this book, you'll discover that many phobias stem from events that may not even be present in your conscious mind. In a defining moment, your brain established a connection between fear or danger and a specific experience. Imagine being trapped in a confined space and your brain questioning, 'How does this make me feel?' If the answer is 'afraid', the brain instantly forms an association that all small spaces equate to fear. From then on, whenever you encounter a tight space that same fearful response is triggered.

Phobias engage various regions of the brain, each playing a role in the formation and perpetuation of irrational fears. This process is important for both the creation and the transformation of a phobia. So, let's take a closer look at the science behind what's occurring in your brain.

Sensory input or stimulus

Our brain has a sophisticated system that detects potential threats in our environment through our senses. This system collects information through our sight, hearing, touch, smell and taste and determines if there's a potential danger. For example, if you have a snake phobia, your sensory input system may detect a visual cue of a snake-like object and trigger a fear response, even if it turns out to be just a harmless length of rope. This trigger activates a series of physiological reactions that make up the fear response, as we'll cover in more detail in Step 4. However, it's important to note that our sensory input system is not always accurate and may sometimes perceive non-threatening stimuli as a threat.

Imagine the various parts of your brain are characters in a heist movie. The sensory input system is the lookout. Just as the lookout in a movie keeps an eye out for potential threats, the sensory input system detects potential dangers in the environment. When a threat is perceived, the lookout alerts the team and a plan is put into action. Similarly, the sensory input system triggers the fear response.

The amygdala

Imagine the amygdala as the mastermind in our heist movie scenario. Orchestrating a high-stakes operation, the amygdala efficiently scans your surroundings, identifying potential threats and swiftly signalling your body to prepare for action. Nestled deep within your temporal lobes, this almond-shaped gem is an integral part of the limbic system that governs emotions, memory and survival instincts.

When you encounter a perceived danger or negative stimulus, the amygdala leaps into action like a seasoned pro, adeptly processing sensory information and activating the fear response. It guides your behaviour using instinctual reflexes honed from lessons learned throughout your life. Because of this, the amygdala often takes charge, making decisions before the rest of your mind even knows what's happening. This heightened sensitivity can sometimes lead to overreactions, especially when it comes to phobias. In such cases, your amygdala may trigger a powerful fear response to a harmless stimulus, like in the above example of mistaking a rope for a snake, and can cause intense anxiety or distress. But remember, the amygdala's primary purpose is to protect you. When faced with a perceived threat, this crucial reaction culminates in the stress response – the fight or flight reaction – all in the name of our safety and wellbeing.

Fight or flight

The concept of *fight or flight* was coined by Walter Bradford Cannon, a physiologist who, through research of animal behaviour, discovered how our bodies mobilize energy in response to perceived threats.

In the split second it takes for your amygdala to decide what to do, it kicks off a series of physiological changes designed to help you survive the situation at hand. It prepares the body to react to the perceived threat by initiating responses such as an increased heart rate, rapid breathing and the release of stress hormones like adrenaline and cortisol.

Your pupils dilate so you can see more clearly, your body hairs stand up to make you more aware of touch and vibration, your heart beats faster so that more blood is pumped around your body to support your organs, and your breathing speeds up to allow more oxygen into your lungs, nose and throat, helping your limbs work harder.

The choices your amygdala gives you are fight, flight, freeze and sometimes fawn. In our heist movie, they are our crew members. In the face of unknown threat – for example, hearing movement behind you – your crew has a few options:

Fight (the muscle): You decide to confront the source of the noise. Like the crew's muscle, you're ready for action. You grab a nearby weapon, prepared to defend yourself from whatever might emerge.

Flight (the getaway driver): Alternatively, you choose to flee the scene. Like the skilled getaway driver, your heart races, adrenaline surges and you run as fast as you can in the opposite direction, seeking safety.

Freeze (the stealth expert): Instead of fighting or fleeing, your body freezes in place. Like a stealth expert, you hope that by remaining still and silent the potential threat won't notice you and will pass by without incident.

While there are other fear or stress responses, they tend to involve types of appeasement and are often more relevant to social situations. Thus, we can group them here as:

Fawn (the smooth talker): In this response, you attempt to appease the potential threat, like the crew's smooth talker. If the noise turns out to be a security guard, you might try to speak in a soothing tone to distract them or try to charm them into letting the team pass in hopes of calming it down and avoiding harm.

So why do we have these automatic responses? Well, imagine you're a prehistoric human out hunting and you see a sabre-toothed tiger nearby. You've got a split second to decide what to do, because if you take too long the tiger will eat you. The brain doesn't try to fish out memories of other times you saw a tiger, and it doesn't ask for statistics on tiger encounter survival rates or the relative speed of tigers and humans. It simply reacts.

These possible responses to danger – to fight, to run away or to play dead – are nature's oldest and most potent survival strategy. They are all incredibly useful responses when you're facing a sabre-toothed tiger; they're less useful when you're speaking in public or dealing with a house spider. Nevertheless, those possible responses to danger still often show up in these situations.

In a modern setting, the fear or stress response might look different for someone with glossophobia (fear of public speaking). You don't start trying to attack your audience or lie on the floor pretending you're dead. Instead:

In **fight** mode, you might become defensive or argumentative, try to over-justify your points or become overly loud or impatient with your audience's questions.

In **flight** mode, you might avoid any situation that requires public speaking, resort to excessive pacing or overly dramatic movements, make excuses to leave the stage or even cancel your presentation altogether.

In **freeze** mode, you might experience stage fright or be unable to speak, your voice may start to crack or become high pitched. Or, you might lose focus and forget what you planned to say.

In **fawn** mode, you may aim to avoid criticism or rejection by agreeing with the audience, pleasing them and overusing self-deprecation.

For arachnophobia (fear of spiders), these responses might manifest as follows:

In **fight** mode, you might try to kill the spider, yell at it or use an object to remove it from your vicinity.

In **flight** mode, you might run away from the spider, leave the room, seek refuge or jump up onto a chair.

In **freeze** mode, you might become paralyzed with fear and be unable to move or react at all.

Although these reactions are instinctual and are meant to protect us from danger, they aren't helpful in situations involving irrational fears, where danger isn't really present.

Our fear or stress response may vary depending on the situation, but often we have a preferred or dominant response. Different stress responses within a group can impact others too, leading to a cycle of escalating or de-escalating reactions.

For example, consider a couple facing a problem. Person I has a fight response and starts jumping up and down, insisting that they need to solve the issue immediately. Meanwhile, Person 2 has a freeze response and stands still, not moving. As a result, Person I's fight response becomes more frantic, which in turn increases Person 2's freeze response.

EXERCISE:

Reflect on stressful or fearful situations in your life and determine which stress response you most often resort to: fight, flight, freeze or fawn. Now, think about key people in your life – this could be at work, at home or in relationships – and consider what their go-to stress responses are. Analyze how the stress responses of others might increase or decrease your own stress response and how yours might impact them.

Knowing this can improve your communication and problem-solving skills in stressful situations.

The hippocampus

Next, we have the hippocampus. As the strategist in our heist movie scenario, it is responsible for processing and storing memories related to past experiences, including the fearful ones. The hippocampus evaluates past experiences and provides invaluable context for future encounters with similar situations, helping us adapt and plan accordingly.

The hippocampus is a part of the limbic system, which is located in the medial temporal lobe of the brain. It is situated deep inside the brain and is shaped like a seahorse. It is a memory specialist, preserving the recollections in your brain by connecting emotions and sensations to create enduring memories. However, when it comes to phobias, the hippocampus can construct a persuasive narrative that sustains irrational fears.

When you encounter a fearful situation the hippocampus kicks in, processing information from past experiences related to your fear. As the hippocampus retrieves the relevant memory, it may amplify the fear response initiated by the amygdala, which leads to an increased activation of the fight, flight or freeze reactions. This can cause the individual to react with intense fear or panic.

In our snake example from earlier, the hippocampus is where memories of past experiences related to snakes are stored. These could be negative or traumatic, so when a person encounters a situation that reminds them of a past negative experience, their hippocampus retrieves the relevant memory. If someone had previously encountered a snake and been frightened, their hippocampus would store that memory and later, when they come across something that resembles a snake – even a rope or a hose and even though the current situation is not dangerous – their hippocampus may dig out the memory of their previous frightening encounter and apply it here.

This retrieval of the negative memory can result in an exaggerated fear response, causing the individual to react with intense fear. We will dive deeper into the topic of conditioning later in this chapter.

Prefrontal cortex

The information retrieved from the hippocampus is then sent to the prefrontal cortex (PFC).

The PFC is the overall team leader in our heist movie. Located in the anterior part of the frontal lobes, the PFC is the key decision-maker in your brain.

It's in charge of deciding on a course of action, delegating tasks to the rest of the team and ensuring that everything runs smoothly, and it is responsible for critical cognitive functions like planning, problem-solving, working memory, attention, impulse control and social behaviour. Think of the PFC as the ultimate orchestrator of goal-directed behaviour. It gathers information from various other parts of the brain and crafts a coordinated response. The PFC processes sensory input and emotional data from the limbic system, connecting with numerous other brain regions to create a seamless, appropriate reaction.

In the face of fear, the PFC is the cool, collected leader who assesses the situation. It takes into account the contextual information provided by the hippocampus and modulates the fear response accordingly. However, in individuals with phobias, cognitive biases can disrupt the PFC's accurate assessment of a situation. These biases are systematic errors in thinking that affect our decisions, judgements and perceptions, leading to distorted beliefs and irrational behaviour.

In the case of phobias, cognitive biases may cause someone to overestimate the danger or threat posed by a specific stimulus, resulting in an exaggerated fear response. Common cognitive biases that might be at play in phobic situations include deletions, distortions and generalizations.

Anterior cingulate cortex

The anterior cingulate cortex (ACC) is a brain region located in the medial frontal lobe, which acts as the emotional coordinator, managing the fear response and evaluating threat levels. This part of the brain is the emotional anchor of the team. It is the part responsible for keeping everyone calm and focused, even in high-pressure situations. It is level-headed and rational, able to diffuse any conflicts and provide comfort and support to the rest of the team.

The emotional anchor is essential to the heist team's success, just as the ACC is crucial to regulating emotions and stress responses in the brain. It plays a vital role in integrating emotional and cognitive information and moderating the stress response accordingly. Through monitoring and adjusting emotional responses, it allows individuals to react appropriately in different situations.

Similar to the PFC, the ACC is involved in various cognitive, emotional and behavioural processes. However, the PFC is responsible for higher-order cognitive functions such as planning, decision-making and problem-solving. In contrast, the ACC plays a role in attention, conflict monitoring, error detection, emotion regulation and pain perception.

In individuals with phobias, the ACC's ability to regulate the stress response may be compromised, just like the PFC.

Insula

After the ACC integrates emotional and cognitive information, the information flows to the insula, which is a region of the brain located deep within the lateral sulcus, also known as the Sylvian fissure.

The insula is responsible for processing emotions, self-awareness and physical sensations, including those related to stress and fear. It amplifies physical sensations related to stress, which can intensify the fear response. In our heist movie, the insula is like the team's survival expert, responsible for making sure they have everything they need to stay alive and complete the heist. They are resourceful and practical and are always prepared for any situation.

However, in individuals with phobias, the insula may increase sensitivity to physical sensations during a fear response, intensifying anxiety. This can make it challenging to regulate emotional responses and may lead to overreactive or irrational behaviour.

Now that you've been introduced to these influential players, you can see they collaborate in a delicate interplay to process fear-provoking stimuli. In the case of phobias, however, this balance may be disturbed, leading to irrational and persistent fears. When our minds and bodies are in reactive mode, it activates what is called the sympathetic nervous system, which is a state of heightened alertness and survival.

The aim of my work, and of this book, is to dial down the overactive sympathetic responses and help to guide the mind and body into the parasympathetic nervous system – the system that allows for relaxation and restoration.

QUICK RECAP:

▶ Sensory input (the lookout) detects a potential threat related to a phobia.

▶ The amygdala (the mastermind) processes the sensory information and activates the stress responses.

▶ Stress responses (the crew members) take action: fight, flight, freeze or fawn.

▶ The hippocampus (the strategist) processes information, evaluates past experiences and provides context for the future.

▶ The prefrontal cortex (the team leader) is responsible for cognitive functions like planning, decision-making and problem-solving.

▶ The anterior cingulate cortex (the emotional anchor) integrates emotional and cognitive information.

▶ The insula (the survival expert) processes emotions, self-awareness and physical sensations – but it may also increase these feelings in moments of fear.

PAVLOV? THAT NAME RINGS A BELL!

As we've uncovered previously, the hippocampus has the power to store negative experiences, leading to a conditioning process known as stimulus response or anchoring. Imagine a moment from your past that sparked fear – for example, a harrowing encounter with a spider when you were a small child. Perhaps you witnessed one of your parents cower in fear at the sight of one or watched a movie that sent shivers down your spine. These triggers burrow deep into your psyche as your brain forms the belief: 'Spiders are dangerous and frightening, and I must avoid them at all costs.' As your brain's primary goal is to keep you safe and secure, it decides to act on this belief, helping you steer clear of potential danger.

From that moment forward, every time you come across a spider – whether you see one in person, spot an image of one or encounter any other triggers related to spiders – your mind races back through your memories (subconsciously and with lightning speed), asking, 'How do I feel about this?' before prompting a reaction.

As a student, I often found that my funds dwindled faster than the month progressed, leaving me in a financial bind. It seemed like every piece of mail carried yet another bill, and I began to dread the sound of the post being delivered. This fear became anchored to the sound of the letterbox, and I began associating it with stress and worry. Even when money was no longer as much of an issue, this negative association persisted whenever I heard the letterbox because, in my mind, I still had that link: letterbox = worry. Fortunately, I recognized this pattern and used a positive conditioning technique to break free from it (which you'll learn in Step 4). Otherwise, that automatic response to the letterbox might still be bothering me today.

Psychologists call these kinds of associations state-dependent memories because what triggers us to recall them is a physiological state. For example, imagine someone gets so drunk one night that they forget what they did. A few weeks or months later, they get very drunk again, and they start to remember what happened the last time they were drunk. The same thing happens for events, places, situations and other things that you have linked to fear, even if you're not conscious of the link. And when you face a similar occurrence in the future (or even just the possibility of a similar occurrence), your mind and body release stress hormones and you feel the same fear again.

Every time this happens, that fear response is reinforced, creating an anchor or stimulus response in a phenomenon known as Pavlovian conditioning.

'Pavlovian' refers to the work of Russian research scientist Ivan Pavlov, and you've probably heard of Pavlov's dogs. Pavlov noticed that dogs salivate when they eat, so he ran a series of experiments to test whether he could create this response at will in laboratory animals. He started by ringing a bell and immediately feeding his dogs. Initially, of course, he would ring the bell, and when he fed the dogs they'd start to salivate. After a while, however, the dogs began to salivate as soon as the bell was rung – before he fed them. With more repetitions, he found that he didn't even need to feed the dogs: they would salivate in response to the bell ringing alone.

In the 1920s, John Watson, a researcher at Johns Hopkins University in the US, decided to see whether humans could be conditioned in the same way as Pavlov's dogs in an infamous piece of research called the Little Albert study. Today, the experiment is considered highly controversial and totally unethical by researchers, but it taught us a lot about how phobias are created.

Little Albert was a nine-month-old baby from a local hospital.

For the experiment, Watson and his assistant put Albert in the middle of a room and then placed a white lab rat near him and let him play with it. Being a baby, Albert had none of the fears and prejudices we feel as adults towards rats, so naturally, he stroked it and played with it. Once Albert was completely comfortable and happy with the rat, Watson added a stimulus. Each time Albert went to play with the rat, Watson would make a loud noise by banging a gong. The noise scared Albert, and, like any small child who gets a shock, he would start to cry. Watson and his assistant repeated the process several times until they were sure Albert had been conditioned.

To test the conditioning, they showed Albert the rat again but without the noise. Each time, even though there was no scary noise, Albert got distressed and burst into tears as soon as he saw the rat. The researchers had successfully made him afraid of the rat, even though the poor creature had done nothing to him. While these kinds of experiments are appalling, what the Little Albert tests show us is that if you expose someone to a negative experience while they are doing something neutral (or even positive, like petting an animal), their subconscious mind takes the negative feelings and associates the whole situation with danger. After that, whenever they are exposed to a similar situation their mind goes into overdrive and its knee-jerk reaction is to try to protect them by any means possible.

If you add enough shock, fear or negative emotion to something, you can go from enjoying it to hating it in a moment. Luckily, this is also true in reverse. Conditioning doesn't need to be negative; the stimulus just needs to be powerful or repetitive enough to make a pattern in the brain.

Many years ago, I decided to embrace the challenge of painting my house. As someone who wasn't particularly experienced in DIY or hands-on projects, I was determined to give it my best shot, calling upon the support of my friends. As we painted, we had the radio on, creating an uplifting atmosphere. I can't remember the exact station but it seemed to have a limited selection of songs in rotation.

One specific song played so frequently during those days that it became inextricably linked to my experience. Even now, years later, whenever I hear that song I can almost smell the paint and feel the brush's texture on the wall. That period in my life wasn't particularly negative or positive, and there was no dramatic stimulus – it was just the sheer repetition and the unique experience that created such a powerful anchor. The sound of the music not only triggers the memory but also evokes the smell and physical sensations associated with it. This demonstrates the power of our minds to form lasting connections.

Any sensation can become an anchor: a sound, a smell, a taste, something you see (like a facial expression or an old photo), a texture etc. Also bear in mind that anchors can be positive or negative, depending on the original emotion, and just as a negative anchor will put you into a negative state of mind, a positive anchor can put you into a positive one. That's something we use a lot in the ICS. Here are some typical examples, some of which you've probably experienced for yourself:

▶ You walk into a room and smell lavender. Suddenly, you're a small child in your grandma's house.

▶ You're outside and you catch the smell of a particular perfume, and you remember a holiday you once had.

▶ You hear a song that evokes memories of your first kiss or a romantic moment with your partner. Just hearing the song brings back all the emotions and feelings associated with that time.

▶ Conversely, there may be a song that played during a break-up, and even though you might not be consciously aware of the connection it makes you feel sad every time you hear it.

So now let's see how that relates to your fear.

THE POWER OF CONDITIONING (AND DECONDITIONING!)

While psychologists have known about conditioning for many years, it is only in recent times that we have created a process for eradicating those anchors.

People often ask, 'How is it possible to create such a transformation, sometimes so quickly, when I've been living with a phobia for so many years?' The truth of the matter is that a phobia isn't really the product of all those years. It's often just one specific event that the person keeps reliving each time they face the fear-inducing stimulus. You see, our brains are designed to learn associations between pain and pleasure at lightning speed.

For example, let's say you've always adored dogs. One day, you experience a traumatic event with a dog. In that instant, your brain switches from love to fear. Or imagine being head over heels in love with your partner, and suddenly you discover they've been unfaithful. Your feelings could shift from love to hate in the blink of an eye.

The beauty of this is that the same principle applies to overcoming phobias. If we can transition from love to fear or love to hate, we can also shift from fear to joy or fear to tranquillity. It's all about finding the right empowering stimulus.

Conscious vs subconscious

When dealing with phobias, there are two areas of the mind we need to explore: the one we are aware of and the one we are not. These are commonly known as the conscious and subconscious (or unconscious) mind, and by 'mind' I don't just mean our head but our whole body too.

The conscious mind is responsible for our thoughts. We use it to try to make sense of the world and it works by utilizing critical-thinking skills, solving new challenges and analyzing different scenarios. This is where we operate from in most scenarios, whether at work, in education or just completing day-to-day activities.

The conscious mind acts as a personal GPS, and one of its key functions is critically analyzing information and situations. Like a skilled detective it guides us along, weighs up the pros and cons of any given situation, considers alternatives and comes up with solutions based on rational thinking.

The subconscious mind differs from our conscious mind as it doesn't focus on rationalizing, problem-solving and logic; it operates below our level of perception. It is emotionally driven, is tied closely to gut feelings and contains thoughts, feelings and memories that are not readily accessible to our conscious awareness.

As the storehouse for the past, the subconscious mind manages automated bodily functions such as our breathing and heartbeat, relies primarily on instinct and internalizes past behaviours, emotions and memories, all of which can influence thoughts and reactions, sometimes without us even being aware of them. It seeks to find the quickest possible means of achieving an outcome, even though it may not be the most helpful.

These two areas of the mind can pass information to each

other. Want an example of this? Think about your very first day at school. You may not have thought about this for a long time, yet as soon as I ask you to remember, it likely leapt into your conscious awareness. The information was tucked away in your subconscious mind waiting for when you needed to recall it.

The key differences in short: The conscious mind consists of thoughts and feelings we are actively aware of. The subconscious mind holds those hidden from our conscious awareness.

Information processing: The conscious mind processes information in a logical, sequential manner and likes to ask 'why?' The subconscious mind can process multiple pieces of information simultaneously. It doesn't use logic and often relies on emotions and instincts to guide it.

Memory storage: The conscious mind holds short-term memories, while the unconscious mind stores long-term memories, including those that may be repressed due to negative associations.

Information management: The conscious mind, with its limited capacity, can hold approximately five to nine items in working memory for about 20–30 seconds, while the subconscious mind boasts a large capacity for information storage and organization. It stores every thought and every memory we have ever had, though most of the time we have no access to it.

Why is this knowledge important when facing your fears?

Have you ever watched someone in the midst of a heated disagreement? When emotions are high, rationality flies out the window and they start contradicting themselves and saying things that don't make sense. If another person tries to bring logic into the mix or highlights a problem with their argument, it usually makes things even worse.

My clients often say that their fear makes no sense, that it's not logical, or they question why they have this fear in the first place. To put it simply – and I'll reiterate this time and time again – it's because *emotions are not logical.*

As we said earlier, it's the conscious mind that asks 'why?' and tries to figure things out logically; the subconscious, however, works at the level of emotion, where fears and phobias are created and triggered, and this is why trying to use logic to overcome a phobia can be slow or ineffective. The conscious and the subconscious don't work in the same way, so trying to use logic to *think* your way out of a phobia will probably not work. It's like talking in Greek to someone who only speaks Swedish; the conscious and the subconscious just don't speak the same language.

Take a post-it note, write 'my phobia isn't logical' on it and put it somewhere you'll see it regularly to remind yourself. If you find yourself stuck in your head or frequently asking yourself why when talking or thinking about your phobia, pause and ask yourself if this way of thinking is getting you any closer to resolving the issue. If the answer is no, then it's a good time to look at your post-it note and explore more useful strategies to change.

To resolve fears and phobias, we need to learn how to communicate with our subconscious in its own language. After all, you didn't cross your arms one day and decide it would be great if you were fearful of something. You are unlikely to have created your phobia using your conscious mind, so trying to solve it logically isn't going to help.

In Part 2, I will teach you how to speak the language of the subconscious mind so you can address your fears and phobias effectively. I will explain how to eliminate the question 'why?' and replace it with words that will help cut through the noise and go straight to the root of your fears.

What's the real problem?

Half the work in resolving phobias is finding the initial trigger – the conditioning event. Sometimes when we explore a phobia the trigger is obvious: being frightened by lightning when you were a child, for example. Other times, the connections aren't that clear or logical. Remember, phobias are a feeling not a statistic, and you create those phobias – that association between a stimulus and a feeling – as a survival strategy.

To complicate things further, the cause of a phobia isn't always directly connected to the event that created it. If, at the exact moment that you were terrified you happened to see something quite benign, like an apple, this can then become a trigger for feelings of shock or fear in the future, even though it wasn't what caused the fear in the first place. This was the case with the Little Albert experiment I talked about earlier. The animals had nothing to do with the trigger sound of the gong, but the fear of the sound became linked to the visual input of seeing the animals.

Understanding the trigger of your fear isn't always straightforward. I have seen many clients who initially believed they had one specific phobia, only to find out later, as we worked through their feelings, that the root cause was something entirely different.

Philip tried in vain to get help from numerous therapists,

counsellors, coaches and hypnotherapists before he came to see me. He had a severe fear of loud noises and thought it must stem from something in his childhood, but no matter how hard he examined his past he couldn't find anything that seemed to fit.

As we worked together, Philip realized it wasn't just any loud noise that triggered his fear; it was something very specific: the sound of thunder. We continued exploring this, and as we went deeper he remembered his grandmother, a very religious woman. During storms she would look out the window and declare that The Rapture was coming. For Philip, this came to mean that every thunderclap was associated with a potential apocalypse. His subconscious mind had transformed the fear of thunder into fearing the end of the world. Ultimately, his fear of the noise was really a fear of dying. Of course, consciously, he had no idea that this was the case.

This just goes to show that sometimes the most apparent source of a phobia is not necessarily the root cause. While, of course, sometimes the trigger is straightforward, other times you need to look beyond the obvious as the true cause can seem irrelevant and we might overlook or dismiss it. Often the reason for this is that things we experience as adults can seem trivial, so we ignore them, but as children they can appear huge, overwhelming and completely out of proportion.

Adults and children perceive reality, space and time in very different ways. For a two-year-old who gets lost in a store, a few minutes might seem never-ending (after all, they haven't lived as many minutes as an adult). Likewise, a small barking dog may appear much bigger or more frightening to that small child. The resulting experiences can leave a mark on the child's psyche, moulding future behaviours and perspectives subconsciously, without conscious awareness. Interestingly, when it comes to our fears and phobias, we tend to react as if we are the age we were when they were created, not the age we are now.

Due to the way the subconscious mind works, even when two people have similar experiences the meaning they derive from those events – their beliefs and feelings or even fears and phobias – can be very different.

You may know the story of two brothers who grew up with an alcoholic father. As they got older, they took different paths: one brother fell into the same drinking pattern as the father while the other brother decided to avoid alcohol completely. When asked why they made these choices, their answers were almost identical. Ultimately, both replied, 'How could I end up any different? I watched my father.' The event was the same, the words were the same, but the meaning was very, very different.

As we will see in Step 4, changing the meaning we take from a given situation (reframing) can be very powerful when it comes to changing our fears.

Cognitive distortions

As you read this book, it might become evident that our subconscious mind often plays tricks on how we process sensory information and operates in odd ways. We receive information through our senses, process it and then data is sent to various parts of the brain, which we covered earlier. Our mind then processes the information through our mental filters, with each filter contributing to how we perceive and react to the world.

The concept of mental filters, or cognitive distortions, originated in the 1960s with the work of psychiatrist Aaron T. Beck, the founder of CBT. Beck identified several cognitive distortions, or what we might call irrational or biased ways of thinking. In the 1970s, the field of neuro-linguistic programming expanded and refined Beck's concepts further.

Deletion: Our selective perception

Deletions help to prevent mental overwhelm and stem from a part of the brain called the reticular activating system (RAS). This network of neurons is involved in consciousness and attention regulation. The brain is constantly bombarded with massive amounts of information – significantly more than it can effectively process. Guided by the RAS, our subconscious mind sifts through this data, deciding what it needs to concentrate on and what can be discarded or deleted.

Imagine your brain as a busy airport control tower with countless signals coming in every second. The control tower must filter out unnecessary information and only focus on what's important, and that's what the brain is doing with deletions.

EXERCISE:

Look around your room and count every object you can see that is blue. Take your time and really look at everything that's there. Do this now before reading the rest of the exercise.

Now, close your eyes and try to remember how many red things you saw without looking around again. Chances are, you can't recall many red objects at all, because your mind was so focused on blue it 'deleted' the red from your immediate memory.

Effectively, the RAS steered your mind to focus on the blue things as red wasn't relevant to the task at hand.

Have you ever noticed something for the first time, and suddenly it seems to be everywhere? For example, if you're thinking of buying a new car, you may be astonished by how frequently you start to see the make and model you want everywhere. This happens because your mind hadn't deemed it significant until you considered buying one – you had deleted that type of car when you saw it until it became relevant.

Deletions are significant when discussing our fears and phobias because our subconscious tends to prioritize data, confirming these fears while neglecting everything else. They can make us overly focused on the things we are scared of and will overlook the many instances where those fears don't come true.

If your subconscious has categorized a specific experience as threatening, it would rather not waste time and energy evaluating conflicting evidence. For instance, if you've developed a fear of spiders, your mind will likely ignore that most spiders are harmless and you're twenty times their size and instead focus on how alien they look or the rare instances of someone being bitten by a poisonous one.

I often ask my clients: 'How many times would you need to be wrong about your fear to change your beliefs about it?'

Let's consider a fear of flying, and in this case specifically a fear of crashing. You're at the airport, watching planes take off and land, one after another, all without incident. How many safe take-offs and landings would you need to witness before your fear starts to waver?

Or how about a fear of dogs? Imagine you're in a park and see a child playing fetch with the family dog. Then you see a dog being petted by its owner and another napping under a tree. How many of these peaceful interactions would you need to see before your belief that all dogs are scary is shaken?

Distortion: The mind's funhouse mirror

Distortion is where our mind tweaks or distorts the information we receive according to our beliefs. It works similarly to deletion, but instead of removing the information it alters or blurs it.

When your subconscious mind looks for an interpretation that fits your existing beliefs, it's like viewing the event through a funhouse mirror.

Has there ever been a time when you woke up in the middle of the night and became convinced that another person – maybe a burglar – was in the room with you? You rush to turn the lights on, only to find it's just your dressing gown hanging from your bedroom door. Tired eyes and the lights of a car driving past your window had created the illusion that it was moving. Your mind distorted the information: instead of seeing a dressing gown, you saw a person, which created fear.

What if someone told you a place you were staying at was haunted? Depending on your belief system, you might distort everyday sounds like someone walking past your room or the heating turning on into believing something supernatural was happening. Your environment, context, beliefs and mind may distort something innocent into something frightening.

This can work the other way too. Say there is overwhelming evidence about a particular subject but a person has already decided they are right. They might distort the information to fit their existing beliefs and be unable to see or accept what might be obvious to others.

Phobias thrive on distortions feeding the fear by reinterpreting events as dangerous. If you have a fear of elevators and you see a sign saying out of service, instead of thinking this may just be routine safety maintenance your mind might distort things into believing the elevator will break down and you will be stuck in it.

And have you ever told someone something and later

discovered they heard something completely different (usually the opposite of what you said)? That was their subconscious mind distorting your words to match their expectations. Similarly, when observing events this mechanism could make us draw incorrect conclusions that may lead us to learn the wrong lesson.

Imagine this scenario if you have a fear of public speaking. You're about to give a talk and you look over at an important member of the audience and see that they don't look happy at all. Now, because you're nervous already, you instantly decide that they must have seen something they didn't like, or they just think you're terrible. You have no idea what is going on for that person or what they are actually thinking about. They could have just received a negative text message, but your imagination fills in the blanks for you and you begin to panic accordingly.

I had a deleting and distortion experience when I moved to a village on the outskirts of London for a short time. As someone who enjoys exploring, I decided to venture into the surrounding woods. The sun was setting, and I found myself in a clearing and noticed a sign saying, 'Please keep dogs on a lead. Venomous snakes in this area.' Needless to say, my mood shifted instantly. I now had to navigate my way back through the woods as darkness crept in, and every step I took, every snap of a twig underfoot, made me jump. I found myself thinking, 'What was that?' at every turn. My mind distorted every shadow and twig into a possible threat because of the sign - it distorted my reality. At the same time, I was also deleting that I was in England, where the most venomous snake is no more dangerous than a bee sting, and alongside this it was December, not exactly prime time for snakes, and any that might be around would likely slither clear of the path. Yet my journey took an age. A heightened sense of caution accompanied every step I took. Every long shadow wasn't a branch but a possible threat. I stepped on a wet twig and my mind started racing. Was it just a twig I stepped on? What danger might be lurking nearby? My thoughts and feelings were being fuelled by the distortions.

After living in the village for a while and taking that route through the woods enough times, I encountered no evidence of snakes, and as my familiarity with the area grew I quickly saw the twigs and branches for precisely what they were: harmless pieces of wood. But it's a stark example of how our minds can distort and delete information, magnify our fears and control what we think and how we feel.

Generalization: One-size-fits-all thinking

Generalization is a process designed to help us learn. The brain uses specific examples to discover how the world works – this is how you learned as a child. For instance, you learned that a flat surface with four legs is a chair and that hot surfaces burn. The generalization process helps our mind take shortcuts; we don't need to re-learn how to sit on a chair every time we see one, for example. However, they also cause us to make sweeping judgements based on only a small amount of evidence.

EXERCISE: ANSWER THESE QUESTIONS WITH THE FIRST WORD THAT COMES TO MIND

People from big cities are...

People from small villages are...................................

Dogs are...

Cats are...

Vegetarians are...

Meat eaters are...

Americans are...

British people are...

Your responses to the above exercise are probably generalizations and give a good insight into how you think about the world. How many of the answers you gave were based on only a few experiences? In some cases, they might even be based on someone else's opinion and not first-hand knowledge at all.

This is how we might meet one friendly dog and conclude that all dogs are friendly. Or in the case of a phobia, you may get chased by a dog once and generalize that all dogs are dangerous, leading to a phobia of dogs.

With generalizations our one-time fearful event can lead to beliefs like:

▷ All heights are dangerous.

▷ I will be judged in all social interactions.

▷ All visits to the dentist will be painful.

▷ I will be scared and panicky whenever I travel.

Now think about your phobia for a moment. What generalizations have you made about it?

The Little Albert experiment I mentioned earlier didn't just stop with the rat. Once Watson and his assistant had made Albert thoroughly terrified of white rats, they introduced other stimuli: a white rabbit, a furry dog, a seal-skin coat and even a Santa Claus mask with a white cotton wool beard. Each time, Albert got distressed and started to cry, just like he had with the rat. In other words, he'd generalized his fear of the rat to other furry objects.

Generalizations are how our phobias can get worse. For example, if somebody had a panic attack in a traffic jam, they might start to avoid large amounts of traffic because of the negative experience. Over time, if nothing is done to reduce the fear, they might start generalizing that all traffic is unsafe, then that driving is unsafe, and this could generalize so much that just leaving the house grips them with terror.

All-or-nothing thinking: Caught in the binary

All-or-nothing (or black-and-white) thinking could also be considered a type of generalization. It is a binary way of looking at the world; things are either this or that, right or wrong, good or bad.

This cognitive distortion leaves little room for shades of grey and little space for different values, beliefs or worldviews. In sports or politics, it can simply be, 'My side is right, and yours is wrong.'

In a business negotiation, the black-and-white thinker may only see a winning and a losing side. Even though they know they might lose, they cannot entertain the idea of a win-win outcome.

In self-perception, all-or-nothing thinking can manifest in a way that people only see themselves as either 'a success' or 'a failure' with no middle ground. A black-and-white worldview is often prevalent in people who fear either one of these scenarios.

If we live in this mindset, it can stop us from seeing the best in life. It can lead us to think we cannot be happy now because we might be unhappy in the future, which, in turn, leads to us being unable to enjoy the moment. We may also ignore any successes or simply move the goalposts to ensure we fail, and our failures become our defining traits.

Using words like always, never, everyone, no one, all or none can be signs of all-or-nothing thinking. Saying things like, 'I never do anything right' or 'Everyone else is better than me' can also be a sign.

This filter affects our fears and phobias and can amplify our emotions. Negative emotions can increase when we view a situation as completely safe or extremely dangerous, and this way of thinking reinforces negative expectations, often resulting in a bias towards negative outcomes. If we believe that anything less than perfect is a failure, we may develop a fear of failing and also a fear of fear itself. You may think, for instance, that if people see you are scared of something you will feel like a failure, which in turn can lead to a phobia of having a phobic response. This can then start a spiral of avoidant behaviours which only reinforce the fear.

If we see situations as entirely negative or threatening, we may also avoid experiences that could challenge and disprove that. Uncertainty is typically associated with both positive and negative outcomes; however, black-and-white thinking causes people to perceive *any uncertainty* as entirely negative, heightening their fear.

This way of thinking doesn't only affect the creation of phobias; it can also limit how a person tries to deal with their fear. For example, it can reinforce the belief that change is impossible with phrases like, 'This is just who I am' or 'I'll always be this way.' It's the idea that if you're fearful for a short period of time, you believe it will never end. When you think about facing your fear, you imagine you'll be trapped with this emotion forever.

The other way it limits our resolve is the fear of making a mistake or being disappointed (fear of failure): for instance, 'If I try to overcome my fear but do not succeed I'll feel like a failure, so it's better not to try.' Perfection syndrome can also play a part: 'If my fear isn't at zero and I cannot 100 per cent guarantee I will not feel any negative emotions at any point in future, then I will not consider facing my fear.'

Black-and-white thinking ignores the natural flow of emotions and that our fears aren't fixed. It assumes emotions will always be the same or that you must be perfect before attempting to solve them. This way of thinking discounts the incremental progress and small wins that, taken over a longer time frame, will compound and contribute to long-term change and happiness.

Let's say you were writing a novel. What would happen if every time you wrote something down that wasn't completely perfect, you just deleted it and started again? How long would it take to write that book? Instead, what if you wrote down your ideas, fleshed them out, then took a break and reviewed them again the next day? Maybe you even give it to a friend to read, and with each review you improve it. Which would get you closer to a completed novel you were happy with? Which method is more effective?

The same goes for learning to overcome your fears because, as the saying goes, 'There is no failure, only feedback.'

Learning mental flexibility

Deletions, distortions, generalizations and all-or-nothing thinking are the mind's way of simplifying a complex world into manageable chunks to help us make faster decisions. After all, our mind's first goal is to keep us safe, and the shortcuts of these cognitive distortions help us do just that. However, as we have discovered, they can also create and reinforce our fears and phobias.

Suppose a person has a fear of heights and their mind then generalizes that all high places are unsafe. In the future, if they have the opportunity to visit a rooftop garden their mind may disregard how secure the balcony is (deletion) and distort any hint of danger, like a tiny breeze, making the rooftop unsafe. They believe that being up high is always dangerous and that being on the ground is much safer (all-or-nothing thinking). They cannot perceive any shades of grey, such as the reality that many people live in tall buildings and are perfectly fine.

EXERCISE:

Next time you have a conversation with someone, notice how many cognitive distortions appear in their language and start spotting when you're doing the same.

Think about your phobia and consider the following questions:

- What cognitive distortions am I using when I feel fearful?

- What am I deleting?

- Is there something I'm distorting?

- Am I generalizing based on limited information?

- Am I using black-and-white thinking?

Then ask yourself, 'What could I start doing differently to reduce them in my thinking?'

As you'll discover in Part 2, a key part of overcoming phobias is being mentally flexible. This involves recognizing our brain's patterns, challenging them and creating new, more helpful thoughts and emotions.

Your brain's misunderstanding

As you can see from what I've just described, your phobia is actually a misunderstanding on the part of your subconscious mind, tricking your brain into believing danger is present when it isn't. The key to overcoming your phobia is not talking down to yourself, beating yourself up or trying to fight with your emotions. As we'll see later in this book, the most effective and lasting way to overcome phobias is to retrain your brain to change the overactive danger response.

My first video on YouTube was the '7-minute flying phobia cure'. I was working with Louise, a client who'd had a fear of flying for twenty years. Together, we tracked her phobia back to childhood and the first time she felt this fear. She remembered her parents getting agitated and anxious about a flight. They rushed around, ensuring they were travel ready and had all the necessary details and addresses. They weren't scared; they just wanted to be on holiday, not waiting at the airport. Last-minute packing and checks seem minor to an adult, but in her mind child Louise created a link to danger, leading her to thinking that 'flying is dangerous'.

Unknowingly, her subconscious held on to that belief as she grew older, so she always looked at planes as something to fear. Once Louise realized this and could look back from an adult perspective, it was easy to change the belief and she completely let go of the fear. When I caught up with her a few years later, Louise could not wait to get on a plane and go travelling. She said she would be going on holiday every week if she could. This example shows you the the power of changing subconscious beliefs.

You can watch the session and the follow-up here.

THE DIFFERENCES BETWEEN FEAR, PHOBIAS, STRESS AND ANXIETY

While fear, phobias, stress and anxiety can be similar, and people can often use these terms interchangeably, there are key differences between each.

Fear is an instinct that has evolved over millions of years to protect us from immediate danger. It works like a car's automatic braking system and stops us when we encounter dangerous situations. Fear doesn't normally stop us, but it gives us pause for thought. It can also be considered an appropriate response to danger in certain contexts, as it keeps us safe and helps us avoid threats.

On the other hand, **phobias** are excessive feelings of fear towards objects or situations that are unlikely to cause us any harm. Phobias are generally caused by a one-time event – a context-specific phobia. Phobias trigger an automatic response, and there is very little thought between seeing or imagining the thing that scares you and your emotional response to it. Think of it like a stuck accelerator pedal, activated without any triggers or rational basis.

Anxiety continuously misguides you, like a navigation system without any distinct rationale. Anxiety differs from fear and phobias because no single event made your brain think, 'Oh, this is dangerous.' Instead, it's caused by a series of experiences over time. Rather than being associated with one specific occurrence, like a context-specific phobia, these are known as complex phobias since they continually linger and tend to stem from prolonged fear or stress.

For example, imagine someone going through a turbulent period in their life: a divorce, having a very anxious or aggressive parent, being bullied at school or having long-term stress at work. Because things are happening over an extended time frame, the subconscious mind can't link one specific thing, such as dogs, flying or public speaking, to danger, so instead it perceives the whole world as dangerous.

That creates thoughts like 'I can't cope' or 'I'm not safe,' and soon your fight, flight or freeze response becomes over-clocked and is triggered whenever you're outside your comfort zone. Anxiety is like having lots of phobias running at the same time. You might think they are separate but they all derive from a core belief that you're not safe, cannot trust anyone or need to be always on your guard.

While it stems from past events, anxiety can also result in a fear of the future. Anxiety creates a stream of what-ifs: 'What if I'm not safe?'; 'What if I'm not protected?'; 'What if my fear comes back?' Ironically, of course, these are all fears of fear itself – you're imagining yourself in the future and worrying that you might be unable to cope with your emotions.

If you had a panic attack in the past, you might fear you'll have a panic attack in the future, that you might embarrass yourself or that you'll be so overwhelmed you can't cope. So, in an attempt to protect you, your mind tries to make you avoid things that put you in threatening situations. Fear is a feeling, but anxiety is something you do. The more you worry about worrying, the more worry you create. And then you tell yourself you were right to worry. It becomes a self-fulfilling prophecy and the fear spirals.

The word **stress** is sometimes used by people when they really mean anxiety, as they think it's a more acceptable way of saying it. However, they are, in fact, different. If we extend the car metaphor a bit more, you might think of stress as being like the air pressure in your car's tyres. Maintaining the proper amount of air in your tyres is imperative for achieving peak performance, but being over-inflated could eventually lead to a tyre bursting and being under-inflated might result in uneven tread patterns that decrease fuel efficiency. Achieving peak performance requires some level of pressure, which might come from experiencing certain forms of stress, but it leads to adverse effects when you are overly stressed or if it occurs over an extended period of time.

When faced with specific external pressures, a person may experience the feeling of being stressed. However, the key difference between stress and fears or phobias is that the former builds up gradually over time while the latter responds to immediate triggers. We won't necessarily respond immediately to stress but we will react when the weight of many demands and pressures has reached boiling point - much like a volcano that builds up over time until it eventually erupts.

In contrast to anxiety, stress triggers are more traceable. Stress is caused by existing pressure, such as deadlines, whereas anxiety, as we have said, results from an imagined issue like worrying about worrying. Stress is more temporary and tends to reduce once the external pressure is gone, such as completing a deadline.

Let's look at how these types of fear may show up.

Imagine you have to deliver a speech. For many, the initial sense of adrenalin or fear can actually be constructive, prompting meticulous research and thorough preparation to ensure a successful presentation. This fear is a signal from the mind, a desire to be well prepared and to perform well. However, for those with a genuine fear of public speaking, this scenario is far more daunting. When the moment arrives to speak, the body might freeze, rendering the individual unable to utter a single word or make any movements. This is more than just fear – it's a phobia, a heightened, irrational response to the prospect of speaking in public.

This phobia can manifest long before the event, with the anticipation causing significant anxiety. This anxiety is characterized by constant worrying about potential errors or mishaps, disrupting normal function and concentration on day-to-day tasks. It can lead to loss of sleep and ongoing distress, impacting overall wellbeing.

This example illustrates the nuanced differences between fear, phobia, stress and anxiety:

- Fear is a natural response, a signal for preparation.

- Phobia is an exaggerated, irrational response to a specific situation or object.

- Stress is the body's reaction to any demand or challenge.

- Anxiety is the mind's response, often characterized by ongoing worry and tension.

As you can see, fears, phobias, stress and anxiety are slightly different; however, often, people use fear when they mean phobia or stress when they mean anxiety. For example, when people talk about a phobia of spiders, they often say arachnophobia. In contrast, a phobia of flying is often called a fear of flying, even if the person cannot go near an airplane without reacting adversely. In this instance it should be called a phobia, not a fear.

So, what is the difference between how you treat these

different types of fear? The seven steps in Part 2 of this book will work for fears, phobias, anxiety and stress. The key areas you may want to focus on are:

Stress – as well as dealing with emotional factors like feelings and beliefs, you will also want to look at changing external factors like your work habits, creating boundaries, your sleep patterns and so on.

Anxiety – secondary gain often plays a significant role, as does fear of the future. (Secondary gain is the subconscious benefit of holding on to a problem, which we will look at in the next part of this book. In Part 2, pay extra attention to Steps 3 and 7.) Additionally, with anxiety you will likely have several phobias, so you may want to repeat the processes a few times or focus on the core emotion/belief at the root of your anxiety, which I'll help you uncover.

In this book, I most often use the words fear or phobia; however, after reading this section you may realize that anxiety or stress is a more fitting term for your situation. If this is the case, please change it in your mind as you progress through the sections.

QUICK RECAP:

▶ Fear is a fundamental and immediate response to a real threat, while an exaggerated and irrational fear towards particular situations or objects is a phobia.

▶ Phobias develop from previous traumatic events, while anxiety can be described as a constant state of worry or fear and usually involves anticipating potential future dangers.

> In the case of stress, the presence of an external demand or pressure creates the stress, which will usually reduce once the demand is resolved.

THE IMPACT OF EXTERNAL STRESS AND LIFESTYLE

Earlier, we learned about Pavlov's experiments and how past events condition us to create phobias, and later we'll look at how to turn off these **internal** triggers and rewire our neurological phobic response. However, we need to consider our mental state, consumption of stimulants and what's happening in our **external** world too, as this can also have an impact on our stress levels, and thus on our phobias. Seemingly insignificant events can quickly become huge problems depending on how we feel.

If, for example, you are scared of heights and have six cups of coffee before going to the top floor of a tall building, do you think you'd likely feel better or worse than if you'd had none? While choosing to drink coffee did not cause your phobia of heights, it can increase the chances of a fearful response.

Or imagine you're having a great day and as you're walking along, someone accidentally bumps into you. Your likely response would probably be an apology, irrespective of who's at fault. Now visualize the same scenario if you are having a stressful day, are lacking sleep, have massive work pressure and the weather is terrible. The same accidental bump scenario may garner a very different reaction.

So, what are some of the external factors that affect our levels of stress?

Environment

Experiencing noisy environments, pollution and crowded living conditions can have a big effect on our overall stress levels. Imagine you were at a party where the music volume was deafening, many people were speaking simultaneously and it was so packed you couldn't move. After a while, living in an unsuitable environment can feel similar and it's very difficult to flourish when this level of stress is experienced day in, day out.

Career

For many people, what they do for a living means more than just money in the bank at the end of the month. In some cases it is their identity, and work is where many of us spend a lot of our time. A workplace with constant pressure due to unrealistic deadlines, unsupportive managers or an uncooperative team can result in extreme levels of stress.

Family and relationships

Quarrels with family members or not feeling supported or understood by loved ones can affect our security and sense of belonging. Also, it can be very easy for family life to become just an extensive to-do list, causing us to lose sight of what's important and leading to feelings of isolation and separation.

Upbringing: Nature vs nurture

The question of whether a person's genetic makeup or their environment plays a more crucial role in shaping how they respond to stress is a common one. If you're anxious as an adult, it is possible your parents were also anxious. However, was it learned from watching them when you were young or was it passed down through the generations in your genes? Or could it be both?

Either way, looking at your family and considering how their behaviour may have influenced you is useful.

Diet and exercise

When we talk about our external environment's influence, we often overlook the very basics: what we eat and how we move. Both of these factors can significantly amplify or mitigate our stress responses and phobias.

Diet: Consuming a diet high in processed foods and refined sugars may not only affect our physical health but can also lead to mood swings, making us more susceptible to stress. Conversely, a balanced diet, rich in essential vitamins and minerals, can improve our mood, maintain our energy levels and enhance our ability to deal with external stressors.

Physical activity: Engaging in regular exercise isn't just about physical fitness. Physical activity has a direct impact on our brain's chemical balance. When we exercise, our body releases endorphins, chemicals that act as natural painkillers and mood elevators. Engaging in regular physical activity can provide a break from daily stress, clearing our mind and enhancing our mood.

Life changes and the unknown

Many of us prefer familiar situations rather than unpredictable or unfamiliar ones.

Every change that takes place in our lives, whether positive or negative, brings the baggage of uncertainty along with it. We can feel a sense of grief or loss for what we no longer have, and events like relocating, getting married, becoming a parent, starting a new job or dealing with the loss of a loved one all require significant emotional change. The fear of not knowing what's next and feeling out of control is something that will increase stress levels in many of us.

That said, if we fail to embrace change and take on new challenges and opportunities, we will never develop and grow.

Health

Dealing with chronic diseases and long-standing health problems – whether your own or someone else's – can create additional stress, and in some instances poor health can inhibit your ability to participate in activities that might help you manage stress better, such as exercise. Stress levels can also increase due to health-related fears like white-coat syndrome, which can make every trip to the hospital a fearful experience.

Digital stressors

Constant connectivity has pros and cons, but using digital screens and devices every day can become stressful, and the inability to unplug or feeling like you must always be accessible for work or social media can lead to chronic stress.

EXERCISE: STRESS AND LIFESTYLE QUESTIONS

1. What lifestyle stressors are having the biggest impact on your fear/phobia?

2. What are some simple changes you can make to reduce the impact of these?

3. What do you need to remind yourself of or do more of each day to reduce stress?

THE FIVE PHOBIA GROUPS

Phobias can be categorized into five distinct groups.

Animal phobias

The fear of particular types of animals comes under the umbrella term zoophobia. Animal phobias can trigger avoidant behaviour and intense discomfort just by thinking about or even seeing a drawing of the animal concerned. Arachnophobes suffer from an irrational dread of spiders, while individuals with cynophobia experience a similar sensation in the presence of dogs and ophidiophobes are afraid of snakes.

Environmental phobias

The fear of nature's elements falls under the category of environmental phobias, and situations like being on a high floor of a building or hiking on a mountain trail can cause people with acrophobia to experience intense anxiety due to their fear of heights. Individuals with a phobia of water (hydrophobia) generally feel great anxiety around any type of aquatic environment, which may limit day-to-day activities and hinder travel. People with astraphobia have an intense fear of thunder and lightning which causes them distress during storms.

Situational phobias

Situational phobia refers specifically to fear of a particular environment or activity. Many individuals suffer from glossophobia or the fear of public speaking, which may negatively impact their personal and professional lives. A lot of people also suffer from aviophobia, which is more commonly known as a fear of flying, while claustrophobes are often at risk of suffering a severe anxiety attack by being stuck in an elevator or any cramped space.

People with agoraphobia experience distressing thoughts about being trapped or helpless in public places, while social phobia or social anxiety disorder refers to the fear of negative judgement and humiliation in social scenarios.

Medical phobias

Fear of blood is commonly known as hemophobia and trypanophobia is the fear of needles or injections. Both these phobias can complicate life-saving treatments and routine exams. Some other situations that lead to extreme anxiety in medical scenarios include emetophobia (fear of vomiting at unexpected times), somniphobia (extreme fear of falling asleep), pseudodysphagia (fear of choking) and white-coat syndrome (fear of medical environments in general).

Miscellaneous phobias

Some phobias don't fit into any of the groups above, and in this instance they fall into the miscellaneous category. Phobias like triskaidekaphobia (fear of number thirteen) and catoptrophobia (fear of mirrors) can make daily tasks difficult for sufferers due to fears around superstitions and negative self-image. Even phobias which are often trivialized, like the fear of clowns (coulrophobia), can provoke intense distress and cause people to avoid the circus, children's parties or any other place where they might encounter them.

We will take an in-depth look at the top ten phobias in Part 3 of this book, where we will examine each phobia's roots, investigate associated myths and facts and look at well-known people who struggle with them.

PART 2

Changing Your Phobia

HOW DO WE MOVE PAST OUR PHOBIAS?

This is the part where we roll up our sleeves and dive headfirst into all the practical stuff, and the goal of this section is to investigate different tools and techniques that can be used to lessen or eliminate your fears and phobias. We will examine the powerful seven-step Integrated Change System (ICS) that can bring about a massive shift in your relationship with fear.

Before we delve into that, though, first we need to look at a few things that you may have thought helped with your phobia but that are actually making the problem worse.

THE WRONG WAY TO TACKLE YOUR PHOBIA

Phobias can often lead us to adopt behaviours that on the surface seem to help us cope, such as fact-checking, denial or trying to avoid the problem altogether, all in an attempt to take back control of our fears. But what if these behaviours are part of the problem (certainly if taken to excess), putting us into a spiral of fear and negative reinforcement?

Avoidance behaviours

As the name suggests, avoidance behaviour is where we try to steer clear of what we are afraid of. For example, someone who is afraid of spiders might avoid places where they are likely to be, like the attic. While this seems like a solution, it doesn't help the person face their fear.

This pattern can apply to any fearful situation. Someone who is shy might avoid parties, thinking they'll escape potential embarrassment. Yet, by avoiding these events their fear of social situations grows, leading to more isolation and loneliness. This cycle is known as the Fear-Avoidance Model, primarily developed by Lethem et al. in 1983 and later elaborated upon by Vlaeyen and Linton in 2000.

After a scary experience, people's instinct is to dodge similar situations; however, this just strengthens the cycle of fear, and while avoiding the discomfort might offer short-term relief it builds long-term habits that deepen fears rather than confronting and overcoming them.

I have seen the avoidance model in action with some of my clients. They start by avoiding elevators, gripped by the fear of panic attacks. As time passes, they think, 'What if I panic away from home?' This sentiment leads them to avoid travelling any significant distance, and with each act of avoidance their confidence in handling their anxiety diminishes. If nothing is done to change this cycle it can escalate to the point where they feel trapped, as their mind has generalized so much they are unable to venture outside their home.

QUESTIONS:

▶ How does consistently avoiding your fears impact your overall quality of life and personal growth?

▶ What have you been avoiding that you could face?

Safety behaviours

Many of us have familiar rituals or beliefs we rely on – like wearing a lucky shirt on game day. However, when such behaviours are tied to our phobias they can become a challenge.

Safety behaviours are another way our mind tries to protect us against our fears. For instance, an individual with a fear of germs might frequently apply hand sanitizer. This provides a sense of temporary relief, but in order to get that sense of relief again the person has to continue to run the pattern of applying the hand sanitizer over and over, which can lead to obsessive compulsive disorder (OCD).

Let's think about someone who is afraid of flying. If the airplane hits turbulence, they may grip the seat, holding on to a belief that their grip keeps the plane stable. After a safe landing, they might mistakenly credit their gripping action to this outcome and completely overlook the inherent safety of air travel. Over time, these behaviours can become rigid patterns, with one believing that safety is dependent on fulfilling certain conditions.

Thoughts like, 'Well, I've always done this and nothing bad has happened, so I better keep doing it just in case,' simply feed the problem.

A client came to see me after he realized a problem in his behaviour that was related to a travel phobia. His doctor had prescribed him Xanax for anxiety, and even though he never took it he carried the pills with him any time he travelled, just in case he needed them. They became like a protective lucky charm. One day, he forgot them, and a panic attack ensued. The cause of his panic wasn't the travel, but the absence of his lucky charm – in this case, pills.

These safety behaviours can lean towards obsessive tendencies, and the repetitive cycles give an illusion of control and safety when, in truth, they might be entrenching our fears deeper.

If you recognize these behaviours in yourself, it's important to ask the following questions:

> What are you trying to control with these rituals?

> Do these actions truly grant you control?

> How often do you link your sense of safety to these rituals?

> What's the price of such behaviours?

> Do these behaviours shield you, or do they keep your fears anchored, preventing you from facing them head-on?

Minimization and denial

While it's important not to overdramatize your fear, equally you don't want to minimize or deny it. Some of us tell ourselves, 'It's not that bad,' while others just want to appear brave in front of friends and family, but pretending the fear isn't there doesn't make it go away.

This brings us to a trap called toxic positivity. This is a state where we feel the need always to appear upbeat, even if we're falling apart inside. While staying positive can be a strength, forcing it becomes a mask that hides our real feelings, and when we're dealing with phobias it can be a huge roadblock. By pretending everything's fine, we end up missing the real issues lurking beneath.

So, why do we do this? Maybe it's because we think that showing our fears makes us seem weak, or because admitting our fears will make them more real. In reality, denial is not the same as letting go.

Imagine your car's engine light comes on. You can address it or place tape over the light and ignore it. The latter might provide temporary peace, avoiding an immediate problem, but eventually the engine will fail and you will have a bigger problem. It's the same with our phobias. Putting a smile on your face might be simpler short term, but addressing the fear is the key to long-term change.

Let's remember: being vulnerable, admitting when we're scared or hurt, isn't a bad thing. It's actually crucial for our emotional growth. By always acting *fine* we end up making our phobia symptoms worse. After all, how can we tackle something if we're always pretending it's not a problem? We will cover this in more detail in Step I.

QUESTIONS:

▶ Have you ever caught yourself minimizing a genuine fear or concern? How did that impact your ability to address it?

▶ In what areas of your life do you feel toxic positivity might be present? How can you work toward a more genuine acknowledgement of your feelings?

▶ How does societal pressure influence your decision to either confront or avoid your fears?

Belittling a phobia

Recognizing and addressing someone's fears in a light-hearted way can sometimes be beneficial, and in the later sections of this book we will be doing just that. However, it's important to differentiate between drawing out humour from a situation and ridiculing the fear itself. Dismissing or making light of a phobia can be as harmful as denying it outright.

Imagine a group knows one of their friends has a fear of spiders, and in a moment of jest they might decide to playfully throw a spider towards them. While this may be entertaining for the group, it can be genuinely terrifying for the person with the phobia and is akin to bullying.

Similarly, imagine someone returning from a war zone with post-traumatic stress disorder (PTSD). It would be unthinkable to force them to relive traumatic experiences for the sake of amusement. The same respect and understanding should extend to someone with a phobia. Just because their fear might seem irrational to outsiders, it doesn't lessen its intensity for the individual experiencing it. Belittling or mocking someone's phobia should be seen as nothing less than a form of abuse.

QUESTIONS:

▶ Have you ever been in a situation where someone made light of your fear or where you made light of someone else's fear? How did that feel?

▶ How might someone's reaction to a phobia (either supportive or dismissive) shape the way an individual perceives their own fear?

Excessive information-seeking

Many people believe that knowledge is power. However, drowning yourself in excessive information can intensify fears rather than alleviate them. Imagine a person with a fear of needles binge-watching graphic injection videos, or someone who is terrified of flying obsessively viewing plane crash documentaries. They might think this gives them a deeper understanding of the risks and prepares them for potential dangers, but focusing intently on our fears only magnifies them.

Being informed is undoubtedly beneficial; however, there's a fine line between learning and overwhelming yourself. Endlessly cramming information in the hope that it will somehow filter down to your emotions isn't helpful. Additionally, if you're trying desperately to absorb vast amounts of knowledge to try to face your fears, you're essentially coming at it from a place of stress, so you're effectively trying to tackle your anxieties from a place of anxiety.

If you attend a yoga class worrying that you are going to find it hard to relax, you probably will.

QUESTIONS:

▶ Are you trying to overload yourself with information to cope with your phobia; i.e. are you learning from a place of stress or of peace?

▶ Can you strike a balance between informed understanding and information overload?

Substance use and self-medication

Some people with phobias try to deal with their fears by drinking themselves into a stupor or taking other substances (legal or otherwise) to try to block out their feelings.

At best, this is a short-term solution which also carries the risk of severe and unpleasant side effects. Addiction can develop quickly as these substances influence brain chemistry and can lead people down a dangerous path that further exacerbates the condition. Additionally, when used in excess, self-medication can make it harder for individuals struggling with phobias to build resilience.

Having prescribed medication from your doctor to help with phobias and anxiety is of course sometimes necessary, and it can be helpful as a short-term solution to get you through an issue. But in the long term, it's normally better to deal with the root of the issue so you won't need to rely on anything else as a crutch in the future.

MOST COMMON METHODS

There are many different systems for creating change. Some deal better with aspects of thought and behaviour than others and all of them have their own strengths and weaknesses. In this section, we'll look at these various techniques before we explore the ICS in more detail.

The most common techniques and systems for creating change often focus on just one area and ignore the rest. I am trained in all the techniques you'll read about below, and while they can all have their own usefulness in working with clients, I have found that no single approach has all the answers.

Cognitive behavioural therapy

Cognitive behavioural therapy (CBT) focuses mainly on becoming aware of automatic or catastrophic thoughts. It primarily deals with phobias by exposing the person to their fear in small steps, and the objective here is to learn how to recognize and cope with your fear; however, it doesn't normally eliminate it. Exposure can often be a long-winded and painful process, and in some cases it can make the client feel worse with constant reinforcement.

While CBT doesn't pay much attention to the feelings, history or subconscious triggers that created the phobia, it does offer techniques that heighten awareness of thoughts and strategies to counteract or challenge them, and at the time of CBT's development it was way ahead of other therapies for dealing with phobias. That said, even at its best it tends to teach you only how to cope with your fears rather than how to transform them and let them go.

Talking therapies

Counselling encourages you to explore your feelings by talking and having the therapist reflect back to you from time to time. While talking through your problem can be helpful because you feel heard and gain self-understanding about why you have a phobia, understanding alone rarely creates any kind of long-term change. Counselling can also be a lengthy process, and you may have to wait for an extended period before you see any difference.

Hypnotherapy

Hypnotherapy comes in many different forms and is a broad field, but in general it aims to change your thoughts and feelings about your phobia through altered states of awareness. A significant strength of hypnotherapy in treating phobias is that it taps directly into the subconscious, which – as we saw in Part I – plays a major role in creating and maintaining your phobia.

The downside with many types of hypnotherapies is that unless you first deal with the root causes of your fear, it either won't work or the fear will return after a short time. In addition, hypnotherapy is sometimes seen as almost magical (even though many types aren't that different from deep meditation). The problem is two-fold. If the client sees it as something done to them like a magic spell, they can think they have no responsibility over whether they let go of their fear or not. Additionally, control issues often go hand in hand with anxieties, so if the client feels they will be brainwashed, they are likely to be resistant to this type of therapy.

The truth is, like any tool that works directly with the subconscious, it's not about losing control; it's actually the opposite. It's about getting your analytical mind and your emotional mind to talk to each other so you have real control, rather than the illusion of it that comes from living in your head. Working with the subconscious mind directly makes hypnotherapy tools a very powerful addition to changing a phobia, but only once the underlying causes have been addressed.

Informational events and seminars

You'll often see events advertised as 'Get over your fear of X'. For fear of flying this can be courses run by airlines, for public speaking they might be run by organizations like Toastmasters, or with animal or bug phobias it could be talks or meeting animals at the zoo. These are typically built around facts and statistics about safety, showing the relative lack of danger posed by spiders, for example. In other words, they're trying to change your phobia with information alone.

If your phobia really is based on a simple misunderstanding of the level of risk, then facts and figures may be enough to help you change. However, for many people a purely analytical approach to treating a phobia is unlikely to be effective on its own.

Mindfulness/yoga

Many people turn to techniques like yoga and tai chi, which use physical movement to help you feel calm and centred, or contemplative techniques like meditation and mindfulness. These are useful daily practices for staying balanced and being present, but they don't deal with the root causes of your phobia or the fears of the future that may come up.

Rapid change processes

Rapid change methods include:

NLP: Neuro-linguistic programming is about modelling a person's successful strategies. When it comes to changing a phobia, it uses re-conditioning and dissociative tools to change a person's emotional link to fear.

EMDR: Eye movement desensitization and reprocessing, and other eye-movement methods like brainspotting, use bilateral stimulation through guided eye movements to reprocess and desensitize the fight or flight reaction.

Tapping: Methods such as emotional freedom techniques, thought field therapy or havening involve tapping or stroking on specific points on the body while vocalizing negative emotions and then transitioning to more positive affirmations through self-soothing.

These rapid change methods come from different schools of treatment, but I have grouped them together above because, unlike many older traditional therapies, they can deal with the past quickly and effectively, and when they do work the results can be excellent. I use many tools from these techniques in the ICS to great effect. However, many practitioners of these methods, especially those trained in short courses, don't understand why the tools work or what to do when they don't. If the practitioner only knows to throw a technique at the problem without finding out what's at the root of the phobia, the tool will not be very effective.

What do you choose?

When it comes to your phobia, what's the *best* way to deal with it? As you've probably guessed, no one technique will be as effective on its own, although they can each have a place in helping you to deal with your fear.

Additionally, many traditional therapies attempt to deal with the cause of your phobia by making you relive the negative experience. However, neuroscientists have discovered that if you relive a negative experience from your past without doing anything to change the emotions and responses that went with it, you often end up reinforcing the negative feelings rather than releasing them, meaning you can ultimately make your phobia worse.

So, when looking at the most effective contemporary strategies to address phobias, the methods I have found to be most effective often have several things in common. Rather than solely intellectualizing or rationalizing fears, these methods use tools such as:

- ▶ **Bilateral stimulation:** By alternating stimulation between the left and right sides of the brain, this reduces traumatic memories and reduces a phobia.

- ▶ **Self-soothing or repetitive movements:** Using rhythmic tapping can provide a calming effect, grounding a person and decreasing the phobic response.

▶ **Interconnectivity of the mind, heart and gut:** Recent scientific research highlights that neurons are not only located in our brain but also in our heart and gut, known as the second and third brain. Using this interconnectedness in the right way reduces stress.

▶ **Techniques that connect directly to the subconscious:** Hypnotherapy and guided imagery delve into the subconscious, addressing the root of a phobia.

▶ **Engaging the vagus nerve:** Stimulating the vagus nerve (the longest nerve of the automatic nervous system, connecting the brain, heart, lungs and digestive system) activates the body's relaxation response and changes the phobic reaction.

▶ **Scrambling the visual aspects related to fear:** Visualizing phobic imagery in altered, often humorous ways can diminish their emotional impact and reduce fear.

▶ **Reframing beliefs:** Challenging and reshaping negative beliefs associated with a phobia enables us to view our fears from a new perspective.

▶ **Turning off the Pavlovian response:** By retraining our automatic reactions, simple actions can help reduce and change our fearful responses to the old negative triggers.

▶ **Turning down the amygdala and engaging the parasympathetic nervous system:** Tools that turn down the brain's alarm and shift the body from fight or flight mode to the calming rest and digest state, balancing the sympathetic and parasympathetic nervous systems, are effective for reducing a phobia.

▶ **Using temporal perception tools that change the phobia in relation to time:** Visualizing and repositioning fearful events in a mental line and changing our perception of it reduces the intensity and impact of phobias.

SEVEN STEPS TO CHANGING YOUR PHOBIA

Now, you may be thinking, 'How can we integrate all these methods?' Well, we will cover just that in this section. The ICS amalgamates the best parts of the various methods, strategies and tools that I've found to be the most effective, along with some of my own processes. I'm not claiming to be the inventor of all these methods; I've simply brought them together in a simple system that addresses all aspects of a phobia, so you can finally move past the fear that's been holding you back.

I also don't claim that my approach is the only way to deal with a phobia. Although I find the methods in this book to be the most highly effective, every individual is unique, and any methodology, or any system of belief for that matter, that claims to be the one and only way should be viewed with concern.

Over the years, I've been certified to the highest levels in many of these techniques and am able to train and certify others myself. Becoming a trainer allowed me to observe many practitioners, and I noticed that they typically made two mistakes.

Firstly, they tried to tackle the issue without understanding it. For example, if a client says they have a fear of X or Y, the practitioner often just focuses on that. However, as I mentioned earlier, there might be other causes. Phobias can often stem from other fears, such as anticipatory anxiety or not being in control.

Secondly, practitioners often fail to understand that a phobia is trying to meet a subconscious need – albeit a destructive or illogical one. We'll see later in the book that sometimes your subconscious mind sets up a phobia because it thinks it's helping you and keeping you safe and protected by making you avoid your fear trigger. If a practitioner removes the phobia without ensuring the underlying need is met, the mind will try to find another way to fulfil that need. It's like playing Whac-a-Mole – you hit one mole just for another to show up. The same might be true for your phobia; for example, someone who quits smoking may resort to overeating instead, as smoking was meeting an emotional need which has not been addressed.

Why are you reading this book?

Too often, when people think about their phobia they focus on what they *don't* want – 'I don't want to feel bad,' 'I don't want to feel scared' etc. – rather than on what they *do* want. As humans we move towards what we focus on even if it's what we don't want, so it's always better to focus on the positive thing you want instead.

So, before we go through the seven steps of the ICS it's important that you find out what you want to achieve from going through the process. Answer the following questions to help:

I.   What is your desired outcome after doing the seven steps in this book?

2.   What would you like to get, do, be or have by being phobia-free?

3.   How would your life change if your phobia was no longer there?

4.   What specific actions are you prepared to take to overcome your phobia?

5. What barriers do you foresee in your journey to becoming phobia-free, and how do you plan to overcome them?

6. What does being phobia-free mean to you in terms of your personal relationships and social interactions?

7. What past successful experiences have you had with overcoming fears or challenges, and how can you apply those strategies to your current situation?

8. How would you describe your commitment level to overcoming your phobia on a scale of 1–10, and what needs to happen to improve this number?

9. Can you think of a specific situation where being phobia-free would allow you to do something you've always wanted to do?

10. How will you know when you have let go of your phobia; what will you hear, see and feel?

The Seven Rs to break through your phobia

In this section, you'll learn a systematic approach to overcoming your phobia. Some of my techniques and strategies can be done consciously with your eyes open, and others require you to close your eyes – which I realize is difficult while reading a book. Scan the QR code below to access a range of tools to help you.

In brief, the seven steps in the ICS are as follows:

STEP 1: RECOGNIZE WHAT YOU'RE REALLY AFRAID OF

You cannot get to where you want to be without first knowing where you are. This step teaches you how to pinpoint what's really going on when dealing with your fear by understanding which questions to ask yourself to get to the root cause of the problem.

Here, the focus is on achieving powerful results by owning, not denying, your thoughts and replacing the word 'why' with how, what, when and where.

STEP 2: RELAX THE CONSCIOUS MIND

We spend most of our lives trying to figure everything out and make sense of the world. This is true for daily life, school, university and most jobs.

In order to connect to the emotional mind (the subconscious) and uncover our fear triggers, however, we first need to learn how to turn our analytical mind off.

STEP 3: REWARD FOR YOUR FEAR (SECONDARY GAIN)

All behaviour is meeting some need, however illogical it may seem, and what is now your problem was once a solution. There was a time in your past when this fear response was the best resource your brain had at its disposal.

Very often, if somebody is resistant to change it's because their mind at the subconscious level thinks it needs the problem (a phenomenon called secondary gain). With phobias, this often manifests as a belief that this fear keeps you safe or protected.

In this step, we go through processes that allow the emotional mind to find better ways to feel safe. Once this is done, letting go of the phobia becomes much easier.

STEP 4: RECIPE (DECONSTRUCTING YOUR STRATEGY)

There is a strategy, or recipe, for how we experience everything from happiness to fear. How we feel in the moment is a combination of what we picture in our mind, what we say to ourselves in our head, what we feel, what we believe, our posture and how we breathe. This step covers tools for identifying the strategy your subconscious has developed for your phobia and then scrambling it. Changing the ingredients of this recipe will change how we feel.

For example, you may picture yourself gripping the seat when you think about spiders. You might see yourself as trapped if there is one in the room and so on. What would happen if you changed that picture to one of yourself sitting calmly instead? How would changing the tone of the voice in your head to something light-hearted or comical change how you feel?

STEP 5: RELEASE THE PAST

This step deals with the triggers from the past that initially caused our phobia.

Here, we use dissociative processes, which adjust the way the mind stores time, and bilateral and self-soothing techniques to help remove the triggers from our past events, which leaves the mind without fearful memories.

STEP 6: RECONDITION YOUR EMOTIONS

In this step, we create positive associations to replace the old negative stimulus responses. The tools we use at this point are very quick and can be highly effective.

Put simply: imagine you're sad and somebody makes you laugh. If you keep laughing, you will likely forget what you were sad about. This is a bit like what it feels like when you successfully change your stimulus response.

STEP 7: REALIZE A POWERFUL FUTURE

'What-ifs' and 'yes, buts' are the two most common things we say to ourselves when we have a fear of the future (anticipatory anxiety). 'What if I get scared?', 'What if I cannot cope?', 'Yes, but I might get hurt' and so on.

These are horror stories we tell ourselves, imagining scary future events that haven't even happened but which we treat as though they have. In this final part of your phobia transformation, we process the what-ifs and future horror stories and replace them with positive self-talk and images. We also plan for the choices you can make in a fear-free future.

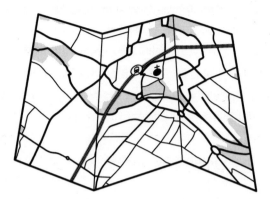

STEP 1:
RECOGNIZE WHAT YOU'RE REALLY AFRAID OF

Recognizing what's really behind your fear is the first big step towards making a change. It's about getting pin-point targeting on what is going on with your phobia by accepting the problem and looking at the What, When, Where and How of your fear.

So often what we think we know about our issue is wrong or only paints half the picture.

Where am I on the map?

When I have some free time, I love to travel out to the countryside and just walk. The more remote, the better for me – it's a great way to relax and come up with ideas. And when I have had enough, I often get on my phone, open Google Maps and find my best route home.

If this has been a big adventure, it can involve quite a journey back. Maybe a few detours and more walking. But when I follow the map, it takes me where I need to go to get home.

Now, if I didn't get out the map and I didn't know where I was, it would be pretty tricky for me to find my way back. Or say I got out the map, looked at it and said, 'Oh, that's way too long a journey to get home. Let me just act like I'm somewhere different.' Maybe I pretended that I was already home. I might feel better in the moment, but there is no way I'd ever reach my destination that way and I could find myself wandering aimlessly all night, no closer to my end goal.

Yet that is so often what people do when looking at their problems, their fears and their phobias. They do not accept where they are on their inner map or what's really at the core of their pattern of behaviour and emotion. When you can accept where you are, however, the next step of changing becomes a lot simpler.

There are several forms of philosophy and schools of therapy dedicated to this concept alone, including the therapy known as ACT (Acceptance and Commitment Therapy). But of course, like all changes, knowing you should do something doesn't always mean that you automatically go through with it.

When I start explaining this step to my clients, I can be met with resistance early on. These are a few of the most common reasons people are resistant to accepting their emotions:

'I don't want to acknowledge it because it sounds so illogical.'
Response: The first thing that I always come back to is to remind my clients that, like we said earlier in this book, emotions are not logical. And secondly, many of the beliefs and behaviours that caused our phobias were created when we were very young and probably way before we had a great level of understanding.

'It's not OK to be this way.'
Response: This feeling can come from the idea that you're not allowed to feel the way you do, that certain feelings are weak or that you will be judged for having them. And, like many beliefs,

this way of thinking can be shaped in early life through events such as negative family and school experiences.

'If I accept the way I feel I've given up or I'm letting fear win.'
Response: This response is coming from the belief that acknowledging how you feel gives that feeling power, but in fact the opposite is true. What you resist persists. When you try to resist, fight or ignore how you feel, it's like doing a tug of war with your emotions. Instead, dealing effectively with your emotions is more like the Japanese martial art aikido. In aikido, the idea is that the stronger and faster somebody comes at you, the easier it is to move out of the way and let your opponent's own momentum bring them down. When you create resistance, it feeds the problem. But when you say, 'Let me shine a light on the issue,' its power dissipates.

Imagine for a moment you were asked not to think of a blue tree with blue leaves. Do not think of a blue tree right now. You're going to be in trouble if you think of a blue tree. You will not think of a blue tree.

Did you think about it, even though I told you not to? Did it get easier the more times I told you not to think of it? You probably found that the more you tried not to think of a blue tree, the more you increased that thought. In the same way, the more you say I shouldn't have this feeling, the more power you give it.

When instead you say to yourself, 'I accept what I'm feeling, what I'm thinking, what I'm imagining, and I know it might not make logical sense but it is what it is. Now how can I change it?' – that's when you have power over it.

Where many of the therapies built around acceptance may fall short, however, is that while accepting your fear is important, you also often need to take the next steps to resolve it and act. If you are still struggling with the concept of being OK with how you feel, then some of the tools later in this book can help.

I recently had a call from a client who felt he couldn't be helped. He had seen numerous therapists for his phobia, but when prompted to focus on the feelings that were attached to it he felt an overwhelming obligation to feel the fear, and in trying to do that he couldn't find it. I asked what he was normally doing when he got fearful feelings, and he said trying not to think of them. When I asked him what he was doing when asked about his fear, he said he was trying to give his fear his full attention. Basically, he felt that these situations were a barrier to working on his phobias, without ever realizing he already had the solutions to his problem. I told him it was great that he already knew how not to be fearful, so the next time he sensed this phobia approaching, he just needed to focus on it, not fight it. He did just that and suddenly he had found a solution, becoming able not to feel fearful in those moments.

Instead of trying to fight your phobia, sit with your feelings and notice everything about them. Sometimes, you'll find that simply being in the moment rather than fighting it can cause the emotion to reduce or even disappear.

Ours is not to reason why

When you're trying to overcome a fear or phobia, it's tempting to ask yourself questions like, 'Why am I afraid?' or 'Why do I keep doing this?' The problem with this is that by asking why something is happening, it encourages you to list all your fears and concerns, so it tends to keep you stuck in the problem. Also, the answers we get from *why* questions tend not to get below the surface of the problem. If you have children, you will often hear, 'But why, but why, but why?' and what is the most common response from a parent? 'Because I said so!' – which is not a particularly satisfying answer for most people.

When I work with my clients, I know they have probably

asked themselves the question 'why' about their phobia many times that week, if not that day, and probably got no closer to a solution. So instead, I ask them to focus on the What, When, Where and How of their phobia. We'll now look at each of these in turn.

What am I really fearful of?

The word phobia can mean many things, from 'I get a little nervous but after a short while I feel fine,' through to, 'If anyone so much as mentions the thing I'm fearful of, I curl up on the floor in a foetal position' and everything in between.

You could look at two people with the same phobia and find that they are actually afraid of different aspects of the same thing. You might think you're afraid of spiders, flying, needles etc, but that is often just scratching the surface of the issue. To get to what's at the core of your phobia, you have to dig a little deeper.

For example, one person with a phobia of spiders may have a fear of how they move:

- The primary emotion the person is feeling is disgust.

- The thought they're having is that the spider might hurt them.

- The initial trigger from the past could be, for example, a horror movie the person saw as a child about killer spiders.

A second person might be afraid of being made to jump by a spider:

- The primary emotions are being scared or feeling out of control.

▶ The trigger for this feeling might not have started with spiders but may have originated from, for example, the person's sibling hiding and jumping out at them as a child, causing a fear of being scared that has generalized over time to include spiders.

These two seemingly identical phobias are in fact made up of different emotions, different triggers and different thoughts. Therefore, the two people require a different focus to resolve them.

Sometimes you can see a direct link from the past to how you feel now. In the first example, watching a film with scary spiders has directly led to a fear of spiders in later life. Sometimes, however, the connection is less obvious, as in the second case. The issue did not start with spiders, it's just that they inspired similar feelings to the original trigger.

To get some more clarity on the *what*, try asking yourself the following questions:

▶ What specifically am I afraid of when it comes to my phobia?

▶ What am I focusing on when my fear starts?

▶ What am I feeling, thinking and imagining in that moment?

▶ What is happening in order for me to start feeling this way?

▶ What am I believing that makes me feel this way?

<u>When</u> did this phobia start for me?

When dealing with phobias, many of the fastest and most powerful tools for change work by finding the earliest memory or event that triggered the negative emotions and changing the mental link between that and the fear.

Trying to find the root cause of our phobia can also be tricky because often we are not conscious of the triggers. It may have started when we were very young and the trigger may seem insignificant through our adult eyes. Often the 'when' of your phobia might be a very small trigger, a conversation, a small doubt, a story on the news etc. You may find yourself wondering how such a small thought could lead to this phobia.

The key is to think of the first event like it's a seed which grows into a weed over time, getting bigger and bigger until it's removed.

<u>When</u> is my fear at its worst?

By asking when your fear is at its worst and when it is at its best, it becomes easier to see the triggers that drive a phobia in the moment. For example, consider a fear of insects:

▶ My fear is at its worst when it's big or close to me.

▶ My fear is at its best when the creature is small.

▶ By comparing these answers, we can infer that one of the key drivers in your phobia is the size of the insect.

Another example with, say, a social phobia might be:

▶ My fear is at its worst when I think the people I'm meeting are of higher status than me, for example my boss.

▶ My fear is at its best when I'm with people who are my friends.

This might suggest that the main driver behind your phobia is a fear of authority.

Take a pen and ask the questions for yourself. Don't think too much, just trust your first answer, and write down all the answers that come to mind. Try not to analyze the answers at this point, just write.

My fear of .... is at its worst when ....

And when ....

And when ....

Keep adding to this list until you run out of things to say. Now write:

My fear of .... is at its best when ....

And when ....

And when ....

And again, keep adding to this until you run out of things to write.

When you're finished, compare the best and worst answers and observe what patterns have emerged from this exercise. What key drivers for your phobia have you noticed?

<u>Where</u> did this phobia start?

The next step in creating change is to find out what caused your fear in the first place.

The first event that triggered a phobia is known by different names in different schools of therapy. It is sometimes called the initial sensitizing event, the activating event or the core conflict, but for simplicity I tend to call it the trigger event.

This is something I spend a lot of time on with my one-on-one clients, using relaxation, mindfulness and hypnotic techniques to tap into the subconscious mind, which we will look at in more detail in later steps. But for now, we are going to work out consciously when your fear was created.

If you are struggling to find the triggers, the list below is a useful guide. This comes from the collective work of researchers such as Aaron T. Beck, John Bowlby, Mary Cover Jones and Joseph Wolpe, who have contributed to psychologists' understanding of the development of phobias at different stages of life.

▶ Early childhood (2-6 years) ◀

Imaginary fears: Afraid of things like monsters or ghosts.

Specific fears: Scared of certain animals, bugs or getting vaccinations.

Darkness: Many children become scared of the dark.

▶ Middle and late childhood (6-12 years) ◀

Real-world fears: Worries about getting hurt, dying or things like earthquakes.

Social fears: Scared of being left out or messing up in front of others.

▶ Adolescence (12-18 years) ◀

Judgement fears: Worry about what peers think or being left out.

Future worries: Concerns about figuring out who they are and what they'll do in life.

▶ Adulthood ◀

Deep thoughts: Worries about life's big questions and the meaning of life.

Health: Concerns about getting sick or family members' health.

Loss: Fear of losing friends and family or breaking up with significant others.

▶ Older adulthood ◀

Aging concerns: Worries about health getting worse, losing freedom and relying too much on family.

End-of-life: Thinking more about death and fearing what comes after.

Of course these are more to do with the natural development of fears at different ages rather than fears that come from sudden shock or trauma, which can be created at any time.

EXERCISE:

Think about four or five key events from your past that may have led to you developing your phobia. What was happening at the time? What were you doing? What were you thinking, feeling and seeing in each event? What are the commonalities between these events? They might not seem to have much in common at first, but you may find that the thoughts and feelings you had in each of these scenarios are similar.

As well as understanding how your phobia started, it's also important to understand what situations trigger your phobia now, since that can give us valuable information about where to focus.

One client, a dancer, came to me for help with her fear of flying. As I dug a little deeper, it emerged that she was only really afraid of flying over water, and as we continued to work together she realized that it wasn't flying she was afraid of, it was water. When she was little, her father had tried to teach her to swim, but he had been pushy and authoritarian, which did not work for a young girl who needed more emotional support. His approach had instilled in her a fear of water that her subconscious later generalized to a fear of flying over water.

If I had simply asked her to think logically about where her fear came from, she would never have made the connection between flying and her childhood swimming lessons.

Here is a quick process to identify your triggers from the past:

▶ Tracing the feeling ◀

I.   Focus on how you felt the last time you experienced your phobia or anxiety.

2.   What did you feel, think and see at the time?

3.   Where in your body is the tension?

4.   Imagine your life as a line and travel back along it.

5.   Go to your earliest memory of having this same feeling. It may not be directly linked to your phobia, but go with it.

6.   What was happening then?

7.   Now what is it you are really afraid of?

<u>How</u> do I do my phobia?

If you had to teach someone how you *do* your phobia, what would you teach them?

We have a strategy for everything we do in our lives, from brushing our teeth to putting our clothes on in the morning to the order we start working. So, it follows that there is a sequence and a strategy that you have to follow whenever you do your phobia: a set of ingredients, thoughts, feelings and behaviours that you have to use to be afraid. This means, of course, that you can also learn how not to be afraid.

Cross your arms and pay attention to how you do it. You've probably done it one way your entire life. Now try to cross them the opposite way and notice if it feels strange or unfamiliar. This is because you've developed a strategy or pattern for crossing your arms. Similarly, you've developed a strategy for your phobia.

One of the first things I ask a new client to do is to teach me how to do their phobia. This enables them to get clear on the 'how' or strategy of their phobia.

Imagine you are talking to an alien that has no idea how to be phobic of the things you are scared of and has also never heard of words like stress, anxiety, fear and phobia. You would have to break down the feelings, thoughts and images that go with these words for the alien to understand.

Now teach the alien what you need to do in order to be phobic:

▶ What do they need to think about, what do they need to feel, what images do they need to make in their head and what beliefs do they need to have?

▶ What is the order in which the alien needs to do things to be afraid, and what would the alien need to do to keep this pattern of fear going?

Now that you have taught the alien how to do your fear, let's consider the opposite:

> ▶ How would you change the order of your thoughts and feelings so they did not trigger the same phobic response?

> ▶ What is the opposite of what you did to keep your fear going?

Now you also have a 'how' for feeling neutral or positive. We will focus more on this recipe and how to change it in Step 4.

Getting to the root of your phobia

Twenty-one questions to deal with the how, what, where and when of your phobia:

1. When you think of your phobia, what specifically are you predicting will happen? What are some examples of the catastrophes that you are anticipating?

2. How negative (0–100 per cent) is the outcome you are predicting?

3. What makes you think this will happen?

4. How likely (0–100 per cent) is it that this will happen?

5. How many times have you been wrong in the past about your phobia? What actually happened on those occasions?

6. When you've predicted catastrophes in the past, have they come true for you?

7. What are the pros and cons of holding on to your phobia?

8. What evidence do you have from the past that your phobia has been HELPFUL to you? (e.g. You avoid something you don't like.)

9. What evidence do you have from the past that your phobia has been HURTFUL to you? (e.g. Because of your phobia, you missed out on doing things.)

10. Are you able to give up the need for control in order to be less fearful?

11. Does your fear really give you control, or do you feel more out of control because you have a phobia?

12. What could you do differently to lessen your fear?

13. Imagine that your phobia no longer exists. How will you feel when the fear is gone? What would you gain? What might you lose?

14. If someone else was facing your phobia, would you encourage that person to act like you?

15. What advice would you give them to deal with it?

16. Where does this fear come from?

17. When did it start?

    a) What are your thoughts about this?

    b) Approximately, how old were you?

    c) Can you think of a time before this?

    d) Did you have this phobia at that time?

18. When you feel your fear, what is your inner voice saying to you? (e.g. 'Something awful is going to happen.')

19. What can you learn from this?

20. What could you do differently next time?

21. What have you learned about your phobia from doing these questions?

STEP 1: QUICK RECAP

▶ Start by accepting what you really think and feel.

▶ Delete the why and focus on the what, when, where and how of your phobia.

- What am I really afraid of?

- When do I have this fear?

- Where was I when this fear started?

- How do I do my fear and how would I teach somebody else to do it?

STEP 2:
RELAX THE CONSCIOUS MIND

Phobias are rooted in emotion and emotions aren't logical. So, trying to intellectualize the causes of your phobia doesn't work, as when you're dealing with emotions the conscious mind can get in the way. Therefore, we need to relax and allow our emotional or subconscious mind and body to do the work for us.

As we discussed earlier in this book, centring processes like mindfulness and yoga might not be enough to remove a phobia in themselves, but they do act as a powerful tool to get us out of our heads and when combined with other tools they can create a powerful synergy. When you relax the analytical mind it makes it much easier to access memories and feelings you wouldn't normally be able to, because while we only have access to a limited amount of information consciously, every memory and emotion we've ever had is stored in our subconscious.

The science of relaxing the conscious mind
There's a model called the 'four states of consciousness',

each one named Beta, Alpha, Theta and Delta. These are known as neurophysiological states. German psychiatrist Hans Berger is credited with recording the first human EEG (or electroencephalogram, a test measuring electrical activity in the brain) in the 1920s, identifying what he termed the Alpha state first. However, the states are sequenced below from the most alert to the deepest relaxation.

Beta is the state of normal waking consciousness associated with concentration, arousal and cognition – on the downside, too much time in the Beta state can lead to stress, anxiety and restlessness. Alpha states are associated with relaxation and creativity, while Theta is linked with meditative states or relaxation. Lastly, Delta is linked to deep, dreamless sleep and healing.

Entering into neurophysiological states has been proven to be beneficial for physical and mental health. Relaxation techniques such as meditation, breathing exercises, self-hypnosis and mindful practices have been widely used as a way to access these brain wave patterns and create a state of restfulness and ease. For example, breathing deeply can engage our autonomic nervous system, the parasympathetic portion of the brain responsible for calming us down, and is known to affect both brain chemistry and physiology, leading to reduced levels of cortisol which is responsible for the stress response. It has also been found to increase serotonin levels within the body, resulting in improved moods and calming our physiology.

The processes below are designed to help you get out of Beta and into one of the other neurophysiological states that create peace and relaxation. You can use any of the exercises listed below before the processes in Steps 3, 4, 5, 6 and 7, and you can also do a process a few times over or combine multiple ones together. Repeatedly doing so can induce a deeper state, known in hypnotherapy as fractionation.

Read through the following instructions several times to familiarize yourself with the process you choose, then try it out. You don't need to master every technique in this section before moving on to the next chapter; you can just find whichever methods work best for you and practise those.

Opening your awareness

Foveal vision is a Beta state where you are focused on narrowly concentrating on just one thing, so much so that you may not even notice what is happening around you unless it directly affects your actions. People often go into foveal vision automatically when they are reading, trying to finish a piece of work or writing an important email. When applied to your fear, this single-focus view actually creates more anxiety and stress. You might even find that during times of single (foveal) focus, your eyebrows are wrinkled, your breath is shallow and your muscles are tight. By broadening your awareness and going into peripheral vision, you can relax your muscles, breathe deeper and take in more information visually.

Expanding your focus to the external world can help activate the parasympathetic nervous system and create a feeling of relaxation. This process differs from our regular day-to-day focus – which is often narrowed to focus on specific details, tasks or worries – because this expanded awareness takes in more of the environment.

To experience this, try the following exercise:

1. Stand up straight, with your feet shoulder-width apart.

2. Smile!

3. Stretch both arms out in front of you and touch your index fingers together.

4. Choose a spot on the wall just above eye level (sometimes, it can help you to focus if you put a post-it note on the wall or choose a fixed object such as a clock).

5. Keeping your eyes fixed on the spot you selected, slowly move your fingers apart, keeping your arms at shoulder level.

6. Stretching your arms out to the sides and looking straight ahead at the spot on the wall all the time, use your peripheral vision to keep both fingers in view at all times – you should find you also start to see more detail of what is around you. **NOTE:** This exercise involves eye muscles that most people don't use often, so you may find that it makes your eyes water. Keep practising and it will pass.

7. Keeping your view wide, let your arms drop to the sides. That view is called open or wide awareness.

8. Take a deep breath in and out as you hold that peripheral vision. Notice that when you keep this raised awareness and stay focused, a lot of the internal chatter and self-talk will start to quieten and dissipate.

9. Relax and return to normal vision.

Now check in with yourself. How do you feel after doing this exercise?

When we use open awareness, it turns off a lot of the mind's chatter, which allows us to take in more information and reduce distractions, as well as being great for getting out of our heads in the moment. It also can be helpful for people with social phobias, like presenting or meeting groups of people. It enables us to stay relaxed and take in more information; for example, if you're speaking to one person, you can see other people without needing to look directly at them.

Safety bubble process

This method helps to turn off the mind's chatter/self-talk.

1. Close your eyes and picture a soothing bubble surrounding you. This is your personal space of safety, where both external noise and internal chatter are muted.

2. As thoughts or self-talk arise, visualize them transforming into little energy forms. Don't judge these thoughts; simply notice them and guide them into a box outside your peace bubble.

3. Likewise, guide any external distractions into the box. See these forms of energy being safely contained, no longer capable of disrupting your peace.

4. Imagine the box being whisked away on a conveyer belt, taking both internal and external distractions away with them, leaving behind only a serene silence.

5. Spend some time enjoying the tranquillity within your peace bubble. Feel the silence, soothing your thoughts and quieting your internal chatter.

6. Gradually let the peace bubble dissolve, leaving behind a calmer, quieter mind. Start to become aware of your surroundings but carry this new sense of peace with you.

7. Slowly open your eyes when you're ready. Remember this visualization and know you can return to your peace bubble anytime.

Progressive muscle relaxation

This method works by tensing one muscle group at a time, then releasing the tension.

1. Begin by focusing on your toes. Tense them as much as you can, hold for a few seconds, then release the tension.

2. Gradually move up through your body, repeating the process with your legs, stomach, hands, arms, shoulders, neck and face.

3. As you move through your body, continue your focused breathing. By the time you reach your face, you should feel significantly more relaxed.

Breathing processes

There are many types of breathing techniques, and they are used in many therapies. While they are not a cure for phobias, they are brilliant for relaxing the mind and body before doing other self-work. There are many studies on the effectiveness of different types of deep breathing. One 2023 Harvard study by Dr Herbert Benson showed that deliberately slowing down our breathing by 10 per cent can reduce markers for panic attacks (hyperarousal) over time due to the reduction of amygdala activation. In addition, deep breathing activates the vagus nerve, which as mentioned earlier links our brain to the gut. The gut is often called the second brain because it has been discovered that it contains over 100 million neurons, allowing it to operate semi-independently and communicate with the brain, playing an important role in mood regulation and wellbeing.

Diaphragmatic breathing

This type of deep-breathing exercise is used to strengthen the diaphragm, a muscle located in the abdomen. When you are focused on breathing from the diaphragm instead of your chest, it helps to increase your lung efficiency and provide stress relief. The technique involves consciously contracting and expanding your diaphragm while inhaling and exhaling deeply. This movement creates an expansion and contraction of your belly, leading to deeper inhalations and longer exhalations.

Diaphragmatic breathing has been shown to reduce tension caused by excessive stress hormones like cortisol. In addition to providing overall relaxation, this practice also helps improve focus and attention, making it useful for activities requiring precision control, such as yoga or martial arts.

1. Inhale deeply for a count of five, focusing on filling your lungs and allowing your belly to expand.

2. Hold your breath for two counts before exhaling slowly while counting to five.

3. Focus on completely emptying the air from your lungs and feel the tension leave your body with each exhale.

4. Repeat for up to ten minutes or until you feel relaxed and calm.

Nostril breathing

This yogic breath control practice is an ancient technique in yoga known as *nadi shodhana pranayama*.

This technique consists of alternating the breath between nostrils. This way of breathing has a beneficial impact on our energy flow within the body, inducing relaxation. The process of alternate nostril breathing activates the vagus nerve, which helps to regulate heart rate and also works wonders for emotional balance by aiding us in releasing stress.

1. Begin by sitting comfortably with your back straight, ideally in a quiet, distraction-free environment. This will help with focus and posture.

2. Using your right hand, bend your index and middle fingers toward your palm. You will use your thumb to close off the right nostril and your ring and pinky fingers for the left nostril.

3. Close your right nostril with your thumb and inhale slowly and deeply through your left nostril, filling your lungs with air.

4. When your lungs are full, close off your left nostril with your ring and pinky fingers, simultaneously releasing your thumb from the right nostril.

5. Exhale through your right nostril slowly until your lungs are empty. Then, inhale through your right nostril while the left remains closed.

6. When your lungs are full, close your right nostril with your thumb and release the left nostril to exhale.

7. Continue this process of alternating your breath through each nostril. The sequence is: inhale left, exhale right, inhale right, exhale left. This completes one round.

8. Aim for five to ten rounds to start with, making sure your breath is slow, smooth and complete, but never force it.

Square breathing or segmented breathing

Square breathing – also known as segmented or box breathing – involves paying attention to breathing in and out through the nose while counting four counts for each segment: inhaling for four seconds, holding the breath for four seconds, exhaling for four seconds and pausing for four seconds before repeating the cycle again. This breathing pattern offers equilibrium between inhalation and exhalation.

I. Gently close your eyes (this helps to shut off external stimuli and allows you to focus on your breath).

2. Slowly start inhaling through your nose. Count to four slowly in your mind as you do this ('one thousand one, one thousand two, one thousand three, one thousand four'). Feel the cool air entering through your nose and filling your lungs.

3. After inhaling, hold your breath. Again, count slowly to four in your mind. Be aware of the sensation of the breath held within you.

4. Now, gently exhale through your nose for a slow count of four, being mindful of the warm air leaving your body.

5. After exhaling, pause for a count of four. Pay attention to this moment of stillness between breaths.

6. Repeat this cycle of inhaling, holding, exhaling and pausing for several rounds, aiming for a minimum of five minutes when you start. As you get more comfortable, you can extend this practice to ten minutes, fifteen minutes or longer.

Remember, the goal of square breathing is not just counting but paying attention to each breath and its rhythm. It is about fostering a deep awareness of your breathing and achieving a state of relaxation and balance. Never force your breath or hold it to the point of discomfort. The counting is merely a guide to developing a rhythmic, smooth breathing pattern. Adjust the count lengths if needed to suit your comfort.

Body scanning

Body scanning is a technique that isolates and relaxes groups of muscles in turn, and it can be used as a follow-on from progressive muscle relaxation. It involves focusing on different parts of the body in sequence and consciously relaxing them. This technique is used in various contexts, including hypnosis, yoga and cognitive behavioural therapy.

I.   Rest your feet gently on the ground, close your eyes and put your hands on your lap.

2.   Take a slow deep breath in through your nose and out through your mouth.

3.   Breathe in as you slowly and silently count to 5 in your mind, 'I...2...3...4...5...', and then breathe out as you again slowly count in your mind, 'I...2...3...4...5...'

4.   Imagine a big, bright, spinning golden light circling above your head and allow it to start scanning your body. As the spinning light comes down through the top of your head, imagine it filling you up with warm, relaxing light.

5.   As the light moves down to your eyebrows, allow all tension to disappear. If you're holding any tension in the top of your head, just let it drain away, then let the light travel down to your eyes and allow your eyes to relax.

6.   As the light continues to fill you up, let it come down to your jaw and allow your jaw to relax.

7.   Allow the light to descend to your throat, and then to your shoulders.

8.   Relaxing the muscles, allow yourself to breathe effortlessly as the light moves to your chest. Fill your heart up and allow yourself to relax further.

9.   If there's any tension left in your body, shake it out as you breathe in the light.

10. Focus as the light travels down into your legs, past your knees and finally into your feet, so you're completely grounded.

II. As you take another deep cleansing breath, slowly open your eyes and return to the now.

STEP 2: QUICK RECAP

This section focused on strategies for relaxing the conscious mind.

▶ We looked at various relaxation techniques and discovered that techniques like mindful practices, meditation, breathing exercises and self-hypnosis are useful alongside other methods to address your phobia.

▶ We reviewed the four states of consciousness model – Beta, Alpha, Theta and Delta – and their role in stress and relaxation.

▶ We explored the importance of breaking away from a concentrated focus (foveal vision) towards a broadened awareness (peripheral vision).

▶ We learned techniques including body scanning, progressive muscle relaxation and breathing exercises. As you work through the rest of this book, if you find yourself overthinking or getting stuck in your head, return to this chapter and use the tools above to help shift your focus.

STEP 3:
REWARD FOR YOUR FEAR (SECONDARY GAIN)

There was once a farmer whose horse ran away. The villagers came to comfort him on his bad luck. But the farmer simply said, 'Good luck, bad luck, who knows?'

The next day, the horse returned with a group of wild horses. The villagers rejoiced at the farmer's good fortune. He now had many horses! Still, the farmer merely said, 'Good luck, bad luck, who knows?'

The farmer's son tried to ride one of the untamed horses, but he was thrown off and broke his leg. The villagers once again expressed their sympathy at the farmer's misfortune, but again, he replied, 'Good luck, bad luck, who knows?'

Later, the army came to the village, conscripting all able-bodied young men to fight in a bloody war. The farmer's son was spared due to his broken leg. The villagers envied the farmer's luck. The farmer, as always, replied, 'Good luck, bad luck, who knows?'

This ancient fable illustrates that whether something is good or bad often depends on your perspective.

So, from our point of view, is a fear good or bad? Well, the answer is it depends. Mostly, people will say it's bad, they want it gone, and they might be doing all they can to let it go. But if there wasn't some benefit being met by the phobia at the subconscious level, then the issue would already be gone.

When people come to me with a phobia, there's often a strong secondary gain, such as safety. The pattern of fear or anxiety is the only way they know to be alert and ready to deal with danger. If you have a phobia, it's because, at some point, your subconscious mind believed it would be helpful and that it served a purpose. This could be the need for protection, safety, avoidance, being ready, feeling important or loved or guarding our sense of identity – even though at the logical, rational level this behaviour might make no sense and is quite likely ineffective at solving the need you're trying to meet.

According to research conducted on secondary gain in the Netherlands in 2004, it was observed that only a marginal number of individuals achieved successful outcomes from therapy when the influence of secondary gain was present.

These conclusions are no surprise. Imagine going to get help for your phobia and the practitioner says, we are going to eliminate your fear. While consciously you might be thinking, that's great, your subconscious might interject, but how will I be safe or ready etc?

It's like someone saying, hey, I'm going to teach you how to be relaxed, but the building is on fire, or like putting down your sword and shield when going into battle – you'd say no way!

While there is secondary gain, as far as the mind is concerned it is unsafe to let the phobia go. Until there is the acknowledgement that the burning building or the battle is simply in the mind, resistance to change is bound to be strong.

Fear: A useful tool in context

Milton Erickson was a pioneering hypnotherapist and psychologist in the 1960s. He was the first person to get hypnotherapy recognized as a legitimate therapy by the medical profession. He would explain to his clients that however destructive a behaviour or pattern may be, there was once a time or a context when it was the best response the mind could find to whatever was happening to them.

A large, imposing man called Psycho came to see me – he was called this by everyone who knew him. I could explain the reason for his nickname; however, if I tell you he came to me for help with anger management, you can likely work it out! He stormed into my office, fixed me with a hard stare and said he needed help with his temper. He then shared that he worked security on the doors at a nightclub.

With my voice cracking ever so slightly, I asked him a question. 'So, hmm, what does anger give you?'

He thought for a minute and said, 'Well, you see, in my line of work it's not a bad thing if the riff-raff is terrified of me.'

Now, he might be right. Anger might be an appropriate response when he's working a nightclub door in the dodgy end of town. The problem was his pattern of anger had become generalized and spread into other areas of his life where it wasn't appropriate, like talking to his boss or interacting with his family.

His anger was useful in one area of his life; it allowed him to feel in control and safe – let's say in about 5 per cent of his life, anger served a purpose. However, in the other 95 per cent, it was detrimental.

And there may be instances in your life, specific contexts when a seemingly negative behaviour is very helpful for you. Unfortunately, our minds often generalize and apply these behaviours across all situations, even when there are no benefits.

For my doorman client, his mind did not want to let go of anger because of that 2 per cent usefulness.

The key was to allow his mind to find improved ways to get the desired outcome: in this case, a need for control and safety. Once his mind was able to find new resources, it allowed him to let go of old generalized behaviour and find more flexibility so he didn't keep going to the same old default mental pathways of anger. As his mind took on these new patterns, I could see the tension start to fade, and his demeanour went from grizzly bear to teddy bear.

Most of us know that living in anger isn't going to get the best result for ourselves or the world around us. However, other secondary gains aren't always so obvious. For example, say somebody has developed impressive attention to detail, honed from years of working as a proofreader. While it might come in handy during their day job, nitpicking every minor inaccuracy in someone's story in a casual conversation at a social event isn't so helpful. Or when a successful entrepreneur has control issues and a fear of train travel. Having control is a fantastic asset in numerous business scenarios, but trying to control a train journey serves no purpose and makes no difference to the journey's outcome other than making him more anxious.

As we have seen, context is everything, and there are times when a seemingly unhelpful behaviour is useful, and vice versa.

Ask yourself, is there a context in my life when my fear could be seen as useful?

Looking back: When fear served a purpose

Another reason we might hold on to fear is that there was a time in the past when this was the best way the mind knew to meet a need, even if that situation has long since been resolved.

For example, a person might have a phobia of being unable to escape from situations and look for the exit any time they go somewhere new. The cause of this phobia might stem from not feeling safe when they were a child. Perhaps their parents were always fighting, so a need to feel protected became hardwired into the child as they used to sit in their room feeling helpless and trapped. If it's not been worked on, they could still have this same phobia twenty years later, as the emotional mind doesn't process time in the same way our logical mind does. Even though they might have their own house and freedom now, their body and mind are still reacting to old information, where being hypervigilant was useful.

Ask yourself: 'How many of my behaviours are being affected by events long since resolved?'

Fear: The preventative power against change

The reward for holding on to negative behaviours isn't always based on emotions. Sometimes it can be financial or a way of avoiding change. Consider a person who is getting sick pay from work and hates their job. It may well be that the person doesn't improve as fast as expected because there is a benefit to staying unwell.

Other times the secondary gain might be changing their current lifestyle or situation. I worked with a client with a fear of flying. I had helped him deal with several different issues but he still could not get on a plane, despite seemingly having let go of all the fear he had linked to flying. 'I don't have the fear anymore,' he told me. 'I don't have the anticipatory anxiety, the fear of heights or the claustrophobia. But I just can't seem to move forward and take the flight.'

As we explored this block further, suddenly he had a eureka moment. He said that his wife had once said to him: 'It's great you're working on your fear of flying because once you're over your fear, we're going to travel the world, and as soon as we've done that, we'll settle down and have a family.' The problem was, he was still young and liked having freedom. In that moment, his brain thought, 'I'm not ready to have a family!' So, his subconscious decided to hold on to the fear of flying because if he let it go, he would be backed into a corner. His fear prevented him from making too much change, even though this kept him stuck in fear.

It wasn't until he addressed the secondary gain that he was able to fly.

Ask yourself: 'What might I have to change if this fear was gone?'

When fear gets you noticed

Sometimes, our minds hold on to problems out of fear, such as fear of losing the tiniest advantage or of recurring past issues.

Compare secondary gain to a warm blanket in a cold room. This blanket (or secondary gain) provides comfort and a sense of safety, even though the room (or the situation you're stuck in) might not be ideal. However, to truly solve the issue, one needs to fix the heater (address the root cause) rather than simply adding more blankets.

Sometimes, clients contact me saying, 'I've seen some of your interventions and they can be very quick, and I've seen your other stuff and it seems you know what you're doing, but you're not going to be able to fix me that quickly.'

The first thing to point out is, I'm not fixing anyone; I'm just here to guide you.

The second thing I say is, I'm not saying it will be quick. Everyone's mind is different. Everyone's causes and reasons for hanging on to their fear are different. But, if it could be quick, why would you not want it to be?

When I ask this question, they often say something along the lines of: 'If it's so trivial that it can be solved so quickly, my issues must not have been significant.' And this is another way our problems can show up: the secondary gain of feeling significant.

You see, people compare notes on who has had the toughest life or who has overcome the biggest problems. It reminds me of the old Monty Python sketch, 'Four Yorkshiremen', where the characters compare how tough they each had it growing up: 'We used to have to get up at six o'clock in the morning, clean the bag, eat a crust of stale bread, go to work down mill for fourteen hours a day.'

Of course, the sketch takes it to absurd levels, but so often people do a lesser version of this, because if we cannot get rewarded for our success we will try to get rewarded for our problems or failures. It's a bit like the second child who cannot get noticed for being a pleaser as the oldest child holds that position, so they become a rebel.

Secondary gain can also be a way your mind gets you love or attention. If as a child you were *rewarded* with a hug when you got upset, your mind can associate having problems with receiving love, and you subconsciously hang on to your fear as a way to get the reward.

A lady who used to love driving came to see me. She could drive for hours, relishing the open road and the feeling of independence it brought. Then, she was involved in a car accident. It wasn't a major one, but something inside her shifted. Her love for the open road turned into a fear that made her heart race whenever she so much as thought of getting behind the wheel. She started relying on others for transportation. She took buses, asked friends for rides and even started walking to places she would've driven to before. People started noticing, and they asked her why she wasn't driving anymore. She told them about her fear, and they responded with care and concern. Subconsciously, she started to find solace not just in the safety of not driving but also in the attention and empathy she was receiving.

What started as a fear of driving had become a means of feeling loved and cared for. This was because she hadn't felt much empathy in her past. These patterns aren't normally conscious. However, subconsciously these patterns are more common than you may think. Especially if in early life the person wasn't being rewarded in healthy ways.

Ask yourself: 'What reward might I be getting for holding on to my fear?'

Fear and identity

Another reason why clients sometimes fight to hold on to their phobia is when it has become part of who they are. There's a big difference between someone saying, 'I am a phobic' or 'I am anxious' and someone who says, 'I am afraid of such and such.'

The first two are statements about your identity, your very sense of being. The third is something you do, and if it's something you do, it's easier for your mind to think in terms of one day not doing it.

When a person is fighting to hold on to their fear, phobia or anxiety, they are basically saying, this is part of who I am and I can't separate my personality from my emotions. When you have had a phobia for a long time, it's easy to question who you are without this fear. However, it's important to realize that your fear is simply an incorrectly learned pattern, nothing more; it's not who you are.

Ask yourself: 'Do I see my phobia as a pattern of thoughts, feelings and beliefs, or do I link it to who I am?'

The impact of prioritizing secondary gain

A common refrain among therapists is: 'The client wasn't ready to change,' and this can actually hold a lot of truth. A person's readiness to accept personal responsibility for their issue can greatly influence the effectiveness of the therapeutic change. However, there's a more empowering view to consider.

Instead of declaring that a client is not ready to change, it's much more useful to investigate what is blocking their readiness to change. Once we discover what that is, the resolution gets much simpler.

When someone with a strong belief that their fear is keeping them safe tries therapy without first working on that subconscious belief, its likely it won't work because their subconscious mind will spend the whole time focused on how they will be safe.

Of course, the truth is that fear doesn't keep you safe, except as one possible choice in the moment that the fight, flight or freeze response is triggered, when real danger is there in the present moment. Holding on to fear from the past is like carrying a bag full of rocks through life with you, and taking it with you into the future just keeps us in anticipatory anxiety; it becomes a whole lot of what-ifs and yes, buts.

As discussed, secondary gain is the belief that hypervigilance and constant alertness to danger somehow makes us more prepared. However, it normally hinders our ability to distinguish between genuine threats and imagined dangers. A neighbour of mine purchased a new car with a highly sensitive alarm system. Initially, as a concerned neighbour, I would rush outside to investigate whenever the alarm went off. However, after a few instances where the alarm sounded without any real cause for concern, such as due to the wind or trees, I gradually started to ignore it.

This scenario mirrors the fable of the Boy Who Cried Wolf. By constantly being on high alert, just like the car alarm, we desensitize ourselves to potential threats. The consequence is that our ability to accurately discern when a genuine threat arises diminishes.

You know how they say, 'Don't decide when you're angry'? The same goes for fear. Both emotions can cloud our thinking, making us react rather than thinking things through. It's actually the positive lesson you can take from that past negative event that serves you, not holding on to the emotion.

Ask yourself: 'How much of my day-to-day thinking is reactive?'

I just need my phobia gone

It's tempting to want simply to get rid of your fear. However, there may be times when that response is still useful, or at least the mind thinks it is. So, rather than just deleting the problem, sometimes it may be better to allow the subconscious mind to find more options for handling a situation, as with Psycho earlier in the chapter.

Imagine you're a chef in a well-stocked kitchen. In this kitchen you have a few basic ingredients, and while you can create one or two dishes with these limited options, your culinary creations may become repetitive. Now, picture yourself in a kitchen with a vast array of fresh herbs, exotic spices, a variety of oils and a wide selection of vegetables and proteins. With such a diverse pantry, you can create much more.

Similarly, when we have a limited range of emotional responses, our mind operates like a kitchen with only a few basic ingredients. All the food we prepare will start to taste the same, and we may find ourselves stuck in familiar patterns. When we cultivate more emotional flexibility, however, we can draw upon a wide range of emotions and perspectives. This enables us to approach challenges and experiences with greater adaptability and creativity.

The real solution is allowing the subconscious mind the gift of choice.

Our problems don't necessarily need to be crushed or discarded. When there is a war, there are always casualties, and it's the same for fighting your own emotions; diplomacy and negotiation will always be better when finding a more helpful way for our minds to meet the needs they're trying to achieve.

Secondary gain can be addressed, negotiated with or even seen as fulfilling some hidden needs. Every behaviour, you might find, is serving a purpose.

ASK YOURSELF THESE QUESTIONS:

▶ What is the belief I am holding on to that keeps the pattern of fear going?

▶ If my fear were to disappear now, I know what I would gain, but what would I lose?

▶ Is there a better way to meet this need?

Fear: A state of perpetual readiness

The challenge with secondary gain is that as you try to address your phobia, as far as your subconscious is concerned you might suddenly risk failure or harm or doubt that you're safe or protected. That said, even if you eliminate your phobia, your survival mechanism is hardwired and so no matter what work you do on letting go of your phobia (the irrational fear), your survival response for real danger is always there if you need it.

Still, some people think anxiety and fear makes them more prepared for disaster or makes them better at their job.

Imagine you're at the hospital, preparing for a surgery. You're feeling nervous about the procedure, so to alleviate some of your concerns you request to speak with the surgeon who will be performing the operation. However, when you meet them you see that they're clearly terrified: they're sweating profusely, and their hands are shaking as they look over your medical charts.

Would you feel like they were more in control? Would you feel safer? Would you be comforted if they told you, 'It's OK; I'm only terrified because I need to make sure nothing goes wrong. I need to be on my guard and make sure I'm focused, so I do a good job.' Would you feel safer knowing they were operating on you? Would you feel comforted by their words, or would it increase your anxiety? Would their fear make you believe they were more in control?

In truth, you would likely feel even more anxious at this point, and if you didn't have white-coat syndrome already, you might suddenly develop it.

All too often, that's what we are doing in our own minds.

Take another example: you're watching a movie and a samurai warrior is deeply engrossed in meditation under a flowering cherry blossom tree, his posture the very embodiment of tranquillity. Suddenly, an ominous figure appears in the distance, disrupting the serene landscape. The samurai, however, remains unperturbed. He gracefully rises to his feet, his gaze remaining steady.

At this sight, would any viewer doubt the samurai's readiness? Would they mistake his calm demeanour for lack of vigilance? Absolutely not. They fully comprehend that his previous state of centredness, the time spent in meditation, has actually served to better equip him.

If part of you still thinks fear protects you, here's an exercise you can do to show you just how much it weakens you instead:

I.   Stand up straight and hold a bottle of water or a weight with both hands stretched out in front of you.

2. Close your eyes and think of a time when you felt confident, happy and calm. Recall those feelings as vividly as possible. As you hold these positive emotions in your mind, try to lift the weight or bottle of water. Notice how your grip feels and how much effort it takes to lift the weight.

3. Next, shake off that memory and instead bring to mind a time when you felt fearful, anxious or angry. Recall those feelings as vividly as you can. When that memory is clear in your mind, try again to lift the bottle of water or weight. Notice if it feels heavier, if your grip feels weaker or if it takes more effort to lift the weight. For the majority of people, it will.

This has nothing to do with physical weakness. It's just that negative emotions make your body and your immune system weaker and inhibit your ability to think. That's why sports people often try to 'psych out' their opponents. If they can make them scared or angry, they've already won half the battle.

So, your fear doesn't protect you, keep you safe or make you stronger or any more ready. It keeps you stuck in the primitive brain and responding like a reptile, not an intelligent, creative thinker with many choices and options. Worse, the more fear you hold on to, the better you become at being afraid and the less able you are to think logically and rationally about a situation.

The fear feedback loop

Often our fears can become a vicious circle and the very thing we are trying to avoid is the very thing we create.

Take romantic relationships. If one partner feels insecure and is terrified of being left or abandoned, they'll often tell their partner they're not sure they love them. They may accuse them of cheating or ask them where they were at particular times. If that happens over and over again, the other partner will start to feel trapped and mistrusted, and they'll begin to withdraw from the relationship. In this way, the very thing the insecure person was trying to achieve (security in the relationship) ends up costing them the relationship.

To relate that to your fear, if the highest intention for your pattern of anxiety or fear is to stay safe, it is worth asking yourself how safe and protected you feel when you're sweating or freaking out. Usually, you'll find that the highest intention has, in fact, created the exact opposite of what you wanted.

But how do you know what is the highest intention behind your actions? When you're experiencing negative patterns of behaviour such as fear, ask yourself, 'What's the positive intention for this behaviour? What does this give me?' Take the answer and ask the same questions about it. Repeat the process, asking these questions about the previous answer until you run out of answers.

The final answer is what we call the highest positive intention.

For example:

What's the positive intention behind my fear? *Fear keeps me ready.*

What's the positive intention for being ready? *So I feel safe.*

What's the positive intention for feeling safe? *When I'm safe, I feel happy.*

Once you've established the highest positive intention for your pattern, follow up by asking yourself whether the behaviour is successfully meeting that intention.

For example, in the sequence above the question would be: 'How happy am I when I'm paralyzed by fear?'

For some people, even reaching that conscious realization is enough to let go of their phobia.

An executive came to see me because his company wanted him to apply for a new role. All he needed to do was sit through the interview, and the position was his. However, he was afraid of being interviewed, and his fear had become worse over the years. As a result, he remained in a role that everybody said he was too good for, and his fear stopped him from growing.

He had tried many different ways to get over this, all without success. However, no one had ever asked the question I asked him: 'What do you gain by holding on to this fear?' Then I reversed the question and asked, 'What would you lose if this fear were to go?' The answer came out of his mouth before he even realized what he was saying. 'I'd lose my ability to be safe,' he said.

I asked in what way avoiding interviews kept him safe. He said, 'If I don't go for an interview, I will not get judged.'

So, I asked him, 'How judged will you be if you refuse to be interviewed, keep playing small and never take risks?' He said, 'I guess I'll be judged more.'

That was the moment his brain realized that the subconscious benefit for holding on to his fear was better served by letting go. That insight allowed him to become open to stop holding on to his fear, work with it and let it go. When the mind can find a better way to achieve that subconscious benefit, it can release the problem. So, it's critical to understand the benefit of your phobia. That is tricky for many people, especially if they are very analytical, as the benefit is almost always not logical – but then, as we've already established, emotions never are.

I worked on another client's phobia over Zoom. She shared that she had a fear of having a panic attack, and as we did the above exercise we uncovered the fact that her phobia was supposed to protect her. 'How protected are you when you're having a panic attack?' I asked her. 'I'm not,' she said. And at that moment, the answer went in so deep that her phobia was gone.

Of course, for most people this realization is not a cure, but it may shake the foundation of their phobia. Sometimes, however, it's not enough to have a conscious understanding, and we need to tap into the subconscious mind.

Mastering secondary gain: Essential tools and techniques

One way to work with secondary gain is to create representations of the resistant part. By personifying it, we create a representation that allows us to have an open conversation with it. We can explore its positive intentions and understand the reasons behind its resistance, and as we integrate these different parts we gradually help the resistant part let go of its grip on the phobia and the associated secondary gain.

Try the following exercise:

I.   **Identify the phobia and the resistant aspect of it:** Identify the part within you that resists letting go of your phobia due to secondary gain, notice where it feels like it is in your body.

2.   **Place the part on your hand:** Imagine pulling that resistant part from your body and putting it on your left or right hand.

3.   **Personify the resistant part:** Imagine that secondary gain part as a person, object or thing. Give it a distinct appearance, form, shape and colour.

4.   **Understand the positive intention:** Recognize that this part has a positive intention and imagine you are talking to it. Use the questions from earlier to get to the highest intention, such as protection, readiness etc. Appreciate that it believes it is providing a benefit by keeping the phobia in place. Thank the part for doing its best to help you even if it didn't feel that way.

5.   **Dialogue and alternative perspectives:** As before, ask the part if it is really meeting the highest intention by holding

on to this fear, then ask it to find better ways to meet the highest intention. Relax your mind and trust the answers that come up.

6. **Observe transformation:** Notice this part may now gradually transform its appearance, symbolizing its willingness to let go of the secondary gain. Observe its shift towards a more aligned representation.

7. **Reflect and integrate:** Take a moment to reflect on the insights gained from the dialogue and the transformation of the resistant part. Place the transformed part back into your body and notice how it feels.

8. **New reality:** Visualize yourself moving forward with this new, empowering way to meet the highest intention and notice how life now looks and feels different.

Exploring unconscious motivations

Another way to uncover secondary gains is to ask your subconscious mind for direct feedback.

In a moment, I'll guide you through a simple technique called the Sway Test. This test is designed to amplify the clues your body is giving to get a yes/no answer using a mechanism called biofeedback – also known as an ideomotor response – which is related to the way you sometimes know instinctively when someone is lying or nervous.

Your subconscious mind is really bad at keeping secrets, and it leaks information all the time through small movements: eye flickers, muscle twitches etc. A good poker player would call them tells. Most of the time, those movements are so small they're hard to see, but if we can make them bigger we can notice them more easily. The curious thing is that even when you're not consciously aware of the answer to a question, your subconscious knows.

Before starting the sway test, if you struggle to get out of your head, it can be helpful to use the relaxation processes in Step 2 to get yourself into a calm, relaxed state first.

The biofeedback mechanism

Imagine holding a long ruler in front of you and holding it just at one end. If you make a small movement with your fingers, what happens? The end you're holding hardly moves, but the other end will go up and down quite a lot. In the same way, the sway test uses your whole body to amplify tell-tale little movements that your subconscious mind will make at your ankles.

At one point in the process, I'll ask you to close your eyes. Just like you did earlier, read through the instructions several times until you've memorized them. As you go through the exercise, allow your subconscious mind to guide the movements. Don't try to *think* your way into it or figure out what would make sense as a 'yes' or 'no' signal: we are simply asking your subconscious mind to let you know that answer any way it wants to.

1. Stand with your feet together and your hands by your sides.

2. Expand your awareness so you take in the whole room and can see left and right in your peripheral vision without moving your head.

3. Take a deep breath in and allow yourself to relax. Put your head back and close your eyes.

4. Ask your subconscious mind – the part of you that controls all your thoughts, feelings and emotions – to give you an involuntary signal for 'yes'. Often, this is a sway forward or back – an involuntary movement that you're not consciously doing or consciously resisting. (For some people it will be a subtle movement and for others it will be more internal. So,

rather than a movement, you might simply feel a sensation like a 'yes' in some part of your body.)

5. You can also ask yourself to increase the effect of the movement 3x as strong.

6. Next, ask your subconscious mind to give you a different signal for 'no' and notice where your body moves.

7. Open your eyes.

That's how easy it is to talk to your subconscious!

If you are struggling, a variation on this method is using a weight on a piece of string:

I. **Prepare a pendulum:** Choose a small, weighted object, such as a pendant, bolt or any other item with some weight. Attach it to a piece of string or a chain, ensuring it has enough length to swing freely.

2. **Establish the signals:** Hold the pendulum loosely between your thumb and forefinger, allowing it to hang freely. Begin by asking the pendulum to show you a 'yes' response. Pay attention to the direction in which the pendulum starts to swing or rotate. This can vary from person to person, but commonly, a back-and-forth or clockwise motion is associated with a 'yes' response. Take note of this movement.

3. **Determine the 'no' response:** Similarly, ask the pendulum to show you a 'no' response. Observe the direction or motion that indicates a negative response. This may be a side-to-side or counterclockwise movement. Remember the specific movement for no.

4. **Ask questions:** With the signals established, you can now ask yes or no questions by holding the pendulum still and focusing on the question in your mind. The pendulum should

start moving in the appropriate direction to indicate the answer.

Finding the positive intent subconsciously with yes/no questions

Now that you've learned how to test yourself with yes/no questions, let's use that to get to the secondary gain. Either standing or with a pendulum:

I. Ask your subconscious mind to confirm the signal for yes and a different signal for no.

2. Think about your fear. Ask your subconscious mind 'Is there a positive intention for this fear?' and notice when it gives you the signal for yes.

3. When your subconscious has found the positive intention or the need it's trying to meet, allow that positive intention to come to your conscious awareness.

4. With the answer you just got, ask yourself, 'Is there a positive intention for X?' and if your subconscious gives you the signal for yes, allow the positive intention to come to your conscious awareness.

5. Repeat the process for each new answer, asking if there is a positive intent and, if there is, allowing your subconscious mind to make you aware of it until you get the answer no – when you do, the last answer you got was the highest positive intent.

6. Ask your subconscious mind whether your fear is the best way to meet that highest positive intent.

7. If it isn't, ask your subconscious mind whether it can find new ways to meet the positive intent in a way that's better for you.

8. Allow your subconscious mind to implement those new feelings, emotions and beliefs. You don't need to do anything consciously; just let whatever feelings you have come up and let the yes signal come through with each new behaviour and feeling it finds.

9. Notice how you feel, and when you're ready, open your eyes.

If you didn't notice a response, or your subconscious mind didn't immediately come up with answers, that's fine, try again later.

As we explore other tools as we go through the steps in this book, if you find yourself getting stuck or having resistance to a process, it's quite possible that secondary gain is rearing its head. If this is happening for you, refer back to the various processes given in this section to work with any resistance.

STEP 3: QUICK RECAP

▶ Fears and phobias can serve hidden purposes in our lives, providing a sense of safety, control, identity or even attention in a concept known as secondary gain.

▶ Fear can sometimes be traced back to experiences where it served as a protective measure. This past context can give fear a powerful hold over current behaviour.

▶ Secondary gain can often act as a resistance to change.

▶ Fear can sometimes serve to gain attention, validation or sympathy from others in a pattern that can be deeply ingrained.

▷ Fear that persists for a long time can become a part of a person's identity.

▷ Fear is only useful when it triggers the fight, flight or freeze response to an immediate threat. Living in constant fear can result in anticipatory anxiety.

▷ Constant alertness to danger does not prepare us better and can desensitize us to potential threats.

▷ Rather than just getting rid of our fear, it may be more useful to expand our emotional repertoire, providing the subconscious mind with more choices to handle situations.

▷ Understanding the subconscious benefit of your phobia can help in releasing it. When your mind finds a better way to achieve that benefit, it can let go of the problem.

STEP 4:
RECIPE (DECONSTRUCTING YOUR STRATEGY)

An old Cherokee was teaching his grandson about life. He tells him: 'A fight is going on inside me. It's a terrible fight between two wolves. One is evil – he is anger, envy, sorrow, regret, greed, arrogance, self-pity, guilt, resentment, inferiority, lies, false pride, superiority and ego. The other is good – he is joy, peace, love, hope, serenity, humility, kindness, benevolence, empathy, generosity, truth, compassion and faith. The same fight is going on inside you and inside every other person too.'

The grandson thinks about it for a minute and then asks his grandfather: 'Which wolf will win?'

The old Cherokee simply replies, 'The one you feed.'

A major element of how your phobia develops and progresses is what you put into your mind.

Our fears and phobias are like weeds in a garden. The more attention and 'food' we give them, the stronger they grow. Have you ever noticed that when you say, 'I have a fear,' people often heap on more fear with their horror stories about the very thing you're phobic of?

Sometimes it's us feeding the weeds ourselves, though. Imagine you're about to take your first solo trip in a new type of car and you decide to research every mishap and malfunction that's ever occurred with this model. Will this make your journey more enjoyable? Certainly not. All it will do is put you into an anxious state.

Just like the proverb above, the food you give your mind – the thoughts, the stories, the images – all determine how you feel. What you put into your mind has a large effect on how you feel. It's about deciding which lens you want to see your issue through.

Your internal recipe for feeling afraid

We've already talked about how asking, 'Why am I scared?' isn't very helpful. Instead, it's more useful to ask, 'How am I creating this fear?' Fear isn't just something that happens; it's a process.

When clients come to me struggling with their phobias, they see their fear as if it's a menacing creature ready to pounce, or an illness they might catch out of nowhere. This gives rise to a whirlwind of *what if* worries and fears. But a phobia isn't something you can catch like an illness. Instead, picture it as a unique sequence or personal recipe you have to run in your mind in order to be afraid.

Creating emotions like fear is much like baking a cake: it follows a specific recipe, and changing any part of this recipe can lead to a different outcome.

In baking, if you forget eggs, your cake won't bind properly. Add flour after baking and it's too late for the cake to form. Swap chocolate for carrots and you'll end up with a carrot cake instead of a chocolate one. Each variation alters the result.

The emotion of fear works similarly. We have a 'recipe' for our fear, even if most of the time we aren't consciously aware of it.

This can include thoughts like, 'This isn't safe,' physical tension, negative self-talk and visualizing the worst outcomes. Alter one ingredient, such as changing the anxious voice in your head to a humorous or light-hearted tone, and the nature of your fear recipe changes too.

Everything you do has a pattern and a sequence, and the more you can isolate your recipe for fear, the easier it is to work on it and change it. Just as you have a recipe for creating fear, you also have one for happiness. For example, you might imagine bright images of smiling faces, feel a tingling sensation in your stomach and take deep, relaxed breaths.

Our internal visualizations, auditory impressions and even tactile sensations are connected to how we feel. If you have a phobia, it's not the thing itself that induces fear; it's our interpretation of it, the stories we tell ourselves, the vividness of the imagery we see and the emotions we feel that create our fear.

Often when a client approaches with a phobia, say, of spiders, with sweeping hand gestures they make these tiny beings out to be the size of a large cat. Fear, it seems, is quite the exaggerator. Bear in mind, I'm from London, England, where the largest native spider you'll often encounter is roughly the size of a small coin. When fear takes the wheel, though, they become massive in the mind's eye, and this is all down to our internal representations.

If we imagine our anxieties or phobias as looming large and close by, they can seem insurmountable. However, by reducing them, pushing them further away in our mental image or even picturing them in less vibrant colours, we can weaken their hold over us.

EXERCISE: QUESTIONS TO TACKLE YOUR FEAR RECIPE

These questions are designed to help you uncover your own fear recipe.

1. How do you know when to feel afraid?

2. What needs to happen for you to be frightened?

3. How do you run this pattern?

4. What is going on in your mind in that moment?

Once, I had a client who sought my help for their fear of waves. I decided to explore their strategy for fear by taking it to the point of absurdity.

We dove into a conversation (no pun intended) and I asked, 'How big does a wave need to be before your fear starts?' The client thought for a moment and replied, 'Probably anything over 3 feet.' I continued, 'So how would you feel if the wave was 2 feet?' The client said, 'Nah I probably wouldn't be afraid of that.'

'How about a wave that's 2.5 feet high?' The client hesitated and responded no. I continued, '2.7?' The client smiled and admitted, 'I'm still not convinced, no.'

'OK, how's 2.8?' He said, 'Yes, that would make me scared!'

'So, the difference between fear and no fear is I inch, then?' I gestured with my fingers to show how small that was, and suddenly the client burst out laughing. He had realized the absurdity of it all. The difference between fear and calmness was merely I inch. By breaking down his fear strategy and injecting some humour, we were able to disrupt his fear pretty quickly. By the end of our session, his phobia was gone.

Time to scramble your recipe

Now that we understand the power of playing with the elements of a fear recipe and have identified the ingredients and steps in your own personal recipe, in the rest of this chapter we're going to start changing your recipe and generating different outcomes.

The ingredients of a recipe for fear are typically:

▶ Beliefs

▶ Mental imagery

▶ Thoughts/self-talk

▶ Posture

▶ Triggers

▶ Feelings

▶ Breathing (covered in Step 2, pages 104–7)

▶ Beliefs ◀

Beliefs can be so powerful that people will fight wars over them. Human history is one long line of conflicts between religious groups, political movements and ideologies.

However, the fact that people will do a lot in the name of their beliefs doesn't make them real. That's why two people can have completely different beliefs about how the world works.

Where beliefs come from

Your beliefs are normally formed before the age of seven, and regardless of what age you are now it's likely you still have some of the same beliefs that you acquired as a child. Many of those beliefs came, not surprisingly, from your parents or other people around you. So, it's useful with any belief to ask whose it actually is. Is it yours, or did you learn it from watching or listening to someone else?

Notice that some beliefs empower us, while other beliefs can limit us. When I was being filmed for the BBC documentary series *Skies Above Britain*, I was talking to the director about what I did. When I started to describe how we create our beliefs, he told me about a stunt pilot they had interviewed for another episode. The pilot had described how, as a child, he had been taken up in an airplane for the first time. In that moment he said to himself, 'I feel so free,' and from that day forward he knew he wanted to be a pilot.

I explained to the director that if instead he'd been feeling stressed that day because of something else that was happening, maybe a test he'd failed at school or a sibling teasing him, and he'd said to himself 'I feel trapped' as he took off, he might instead have made a lifetime choice that flying is terrifying.

The beliefs we create in our early life, if strong enough, can shape our entire future, both good and bad. And with that in mind, it's time to explore what beliefs are holding you back.

What do you need to believe to feel that way?

In order for you to feel afraid, there have to be subconscious beliefs that underpin the issue. As I've said before, most, if not all, of those beliefs are not logical. Just because those subconscious beliefs aren't logical, however, doesn't stop you from having them or being influenced by them.

When I'm working on beliefs, I often ask my clients this simple question: 'What is it that you need to believe in order to feel that way?' When I word it that way, the client will often uncover things they haven't thought of before.

Imagine you're worried about a job interview and ask yourself: 'What is it that I need to believe, in order to be worried about my job interview?' You might reply, 'I need to believe that I'm not good enough. I need to believe I'm going to be judged. I need to believe that failure is not OK.'

Now ask yourself, what do you need to believe in order to be afraid of your phobia, e.g. 'I need to believe that I'm not safe' or 'I need to believe that I won't be able to cope if I panic' and so on. Write down the answer.

We need to make sure you uncover all your beliefs around this, so what else do you need to believe in order to be afraid of X? Repeat that question until you can't think of anything new.

You can also use questions to dig deeper into the answers. For example, one of the answers might be: 'I need to believe I'm not safe.' So, the next question would be: 'What do you need to believe in order not to feel safe?' and so on.

Using these questions to keep probing in this way can quickly get to the root of the issue.

And remember: just because you believe something, that doesn't make it true. In Part 3, I will share common myths about different phobias. Of course, these aren't just myths; they're beliefs that people have about their phobias. But, as you will see in those chapters, they're not true. So, think about the beliefs you have about your phobia and answer the following question: are you confusing feelings with facts when you think about your phobia?

Changing your beliefs: Part 1

Consider news broadcasts on television for a moment. Every so often, a report will highlight the dangers of a particular activity, such as hiking in the wilderness. This report might detail the account of a lone hiker who got lost or injured, and suddenly viewers are terrified of ever considering such an excursion. The common refrain becomes: 'Hiking is dangerous; you can get lost or injured. It's best to avoid it.'

Now, there's no denying that hiking, like any activity, carries its own set of risks. But should we abandon it completely? Should we then also cease driving for fear of accidents? Abandon taking the stairs for fear of falling? Stop cooking for fear of getting burned?

The truth is, life is full of risks, and completely avoiding them isn't a viable or fulfilling option. Yet some of us are more prone to focusing on the dangers. This is largely due to an ingrained belief system, reinforced by confirmation bias.

The important thing here is to challenge these limiting beliefs. Next time you find yourself fearing an activity or situation because 'it's dangerous' or 'it should be avoided', question the origin of this belief.

- Is it from personal experience?

- A singular news report?

- Word of mouth?

- Is it always true?

- Are there counter-examples where this hasn't been the case?

By questioning and challenging these beliefs, you're likely to find a more balanced perspective, opening yourself up to new experiences and possibilities.

Reframing your beliefs

Are you a glass-half-full or a glass-half-empty kind of person? Come to think of it, how can two people look at exactly the same thing and see something completely different? It's down to something Milton Erickson (whom you read about earlier) called framing.

Framing is what allows media companies to put a negative spin on a story to make us feel bad, or a positive spin on the same story to make us feel good. Because the truth is, whether something is good or bad, happy or sad, annoying or pleasing, is all down to the meaning you give it – and you choose the meaning you give to everything that happens.

Erickson told the story of two parents who came to see him about their daughter. 'We're at the end of our tether,' they said. 'She's so wilful. She just won't do what she's told.' Erickson replied, with a twinkle in his eye: 'Well, aren't you wonderful parents, raising your daughter to be so strong and independent.'

There are two main ways you can reframe:

I.   Content reframing is about changing how we interpret a situation. For example, as above with the child who is seen as stubborn. You might initially view this as a challenge, but with content reframing you could see the child's stubbornness as a sign of determination and strength. The situation hasn't changed, but your interpretation of it has.

2.   Context reframing, on the other hand, involves changing the situation in which a behaviour is perceived. Take the same stubborn child. In one context, this trait might be difficult to manage, but in a different context, like if the child's friends were trying to pressure her into doing something harmful, her stubbornness becomes a positive trait that helps her stand her ground. The behaviour is the same, but the context gives it a new meaning.

Both types of reframing help us see situations from a different perspective, which can lead to more constructive outcomes.

Talk to a good salesman; they are masters of changing the frame. They might say something like, 'No, this house isn't small, it's just cosy' or 'It's not badly lit, it's energy-efficient.' This meme is a reframe. Likewise, perhaps the spider you just killed thought you were its roommate and it was quietly taking care of pests in your home. Or the quote you often hear in action movies: 'I'm not stuck in here with you, you're stuck in here with me.'

So, how do reframes work with phobias?

With a fear of flying, for example, instead of panicking when your flight is delayed you could choose to think, 'I'm glad they've taken extra time to make sure everything is perfect before take-off, even though it's costing them time and money.' Here are some more examples:

Agoraphobia: Instead of viewing a crowd as overwhelming, think, 'Each person in this crowd is a unique story. Being here is like being part of a vibrant, ever-changing book.'

Arachnophobia: Instead of fearing spiders, reframe them as nature's little architects, taking care of germ-carrying bugs.

Acrophobia: Instead of fearing heights, you could think, 'I'm like a bird, getting to see the world from a vantage point few can experience.'

Claustrophobia: Instead of seeing a small space as confining, view it as your own personal nest, where you are snug and secure.

Trypanophobia: Instead of thinking about the pain of a needle, consider it as a tiny key unlocking a door to better health.

Glossophobia: Instead of fearing public speaking, view it as an opportunity to share your unique voice and perspectives with a receptive audience.

Reframing doesn't make the fear disappear instantly. However, it is a tool to gradually change your perspective and lessen the emotional intensity of your fear.

Write down some of your negative beliefs and thoughts about your phobia. When you've finished the list, take your pen, cross out each belief or thought and write an alternative, positive meaning below it.

Reframing can also help change how we view our own actions. Take the example of the doorman working on his anger I mentioned earlier. I had him imagine a situation where he was losing control but then added a twist: a police officer or a potential employer was watching. Could he have managed his emotions differently then? Think about this: you're a business owner in a heated argument. If a big client walked in, could you quickly drop the anger and act professionally?

This is useful for those who feel they can't control their emotions or actions. By changing the context, they often find they have more control than they thought.

Reframing is a good start to changing your beliefs. However, it's not always enough, which is why we often need therapeutic intervention processes to fully change those thought patterns. In the next section, you'll get to work on one of those processes.

Changing your beliefs: Part 2

The notion that the eyes are the windows to the soul has long permeated our collective consciousness. Recently in contemporary neuroscience, this age-old saying has gained empirical support, particularly with the advent of bilateral stimulation (BLS) techniques involving eye movements. Numerous studies have demonstrated the efficacy of BLS in altering negative beliefs. Try the following exercise:

1. **Go back to your list of beliefs about your phobia:** Rate the strength of each belief on a scale from 0 per cent to 100 per cent, where 0 means you don't believe it at all and 100 means you believe it completely.

2. **Eye-movement exercise:** Looking straight ahead, without moving your head move your eyes in a smooth arc from fully left, across the bridge of your nose, to fully right, then back. Keeping the focus of your eyes even, without flicking them, like you were following a metronome or pocket watch. Repeat this for a few minutes.
    As you do this, focus on the belief and say it out loud. Notice how it feels to think this thought and how your body reacts.

3. **Circular eye movements:** Keeping your head level, look up as though trying to see the inside of your eyelids and rotate your eyes in a full circle, first clockwise then anticlockwise, ten times in each direction.
    Continue focusing on the belief. Observe any shifts in how strongly you feel connected to this belief.

4. **Vertical eye movements:** Again, keeping your head straight and level, look up, then sweep your eye in an arc down all the way, then back up to the top. Repeat this ten times. Maintain your focus on the belief. Reflect on whether the belief feels more or less true as you move your eyes.

5. **Re-evaluate the belief:** After completing the eye movements, reassess the strength of your belief on the 0 to 100 scale. Reflect on any changes in your perception of the belief and repeat as needed.

▶ Mental imagery ◀

Movies are a staple of our culture. We've all seen characters like Indiana Jones narrowly escaping dangerous traps or James Bond outsmarting his enemies. We understand that these are just stories, not reality. They're scripts, and the great thing about scripts is that they can be changed if they don't resonate with the audience.

Consider the trend of movie trailer recuts on platforms like YouTube. Fans take existing movies and rework them, changing the music, editing the pacing and rearranging scenes to create something entirely different. They can make a thriller look like a romantic comedy or a horror film seem family-friendly. They change the narrative to suit a different genre or to explore new interpretations of the story.

With my clients, I'll often ask them to visualize their fears. What images and sounds come to mind when they think about their phobias? Often, they describe terrifying scenes and noises. With such thoughts, it's no surprise they're filled with fear.

Fear is largely a product of our imagination. When you contemplate your phobia, your mind produces a horror movie, generating frightening images and sounds that make you feel scared – but this narrative isn't set in stone; you can change it. By altering these images and sounds and the sequence in which you perceive them, you can change your emotional response.

So, when you think about your phobia, what do you see and hear?

Changing your inner experience

The images and sounds we create have certain qualities. For example, the images can be bright or dim, still like a photograph or moving like a movie, in colour or black and white. Sounds can be loud or soft, clear or dull, inside your head or coming from a particular direction, they may sound like someone or something specific and so on.

These qualities are known as submodalities. And (going back to our recipe analogy) if we alter the submodalities of the mental imagery we are creating, we can change how we feel. Remember, you have the power to change these elements. Just like a movie script or a YouTube trailer recut, you can rewrite the narrative in your mind, transforming your personal horror movie into a feel-good film. This is similar to how the riddikulus spell in *Harry Potter* works.

As you think about your fear, notice where the fearful image is in your mind:

▶ Is it close up or far away?

▶ Is the image bright or dull?

Now let's change that image.

If the image is in colour, change it to black and white. If it is moving, stop it. What would happen if you made it small: if you made it into a tiny, tiny dot? Throw it off into the distance, so it ends up way off, behind a wall. Take that tiny dot and tower over it like a giant looking down on it. What would happen if you took the image and threw it off into the sun, how would you feel differently now?

▶ What other changes could you make?

▶ What did you notice as you made changes?

▶ What happened to your level of fear?

▶ Which changes made the fear diminish and were there any that made it increase?

Other ways of recutting your phobia:

Public-speaking anxiety: Remember the old adage of thinking about your audience in their underwear? Well, that's a method of recutting. You might also visualize them as cartoon characters or wearing funny hats.

Fear of heights: Visualize yourself being securely anchored to the ground.

Fear of rejection: Visualize the person who might reject you as someone who is very small and far away. This can help to reduce the perceived threat of rejection.

Fear of spiders: You might visualize the spider as a tiny, harmless creature. Or you could imagine it wearing a funny hat and roller-skates or dancing to silly music.

▶ Thoughts and self-talk ◀

Next, we are going to deal with your internal voice: the voice you hear in your head when you speak to yourself. Often when you're scared, fearful or anxious, you have a voice in your head saying things like, 'This spider might be poisonous,' 'This dog is going to eat me,' 'Everyone in this audience is laughing at me,' or 'This car might crash!'

That voice can have a lot of power over you, especially if you're repeating things over and over again inside your head. Still, we can take that power away if we change how the voice sounds.

So, let's do that now.

Place your feet firmly on the ground, close your eyes and become aware of your internal voice.

Think about your fear. Notice what you say to yourself in order to be afraid. Perhaps it is something like, 'I'm not safe.' Become aware of that internal dialogue, that self-talk, and ask yourself, 'Whose voice is that? Is it mine or somebody else?'

Notice the qualities of the voice: whose voice it is; the tonality; the volume (is it loud or quiet?); where it is located (which ear is it in? Is it behind you or in front of you? Is it in your head or somewhere else?).

First, let's play with the location of the voice.

Imagine moving it from one side to the other or moving it behind you. Push it off far away from you until it becomes a tiny, distant echo.

How would that change how you feel?

How would it be if the voice in your head had no gravitas, no power? How much control would that voice have over you?

Let's change the voice and see.

First, make it sound like the most boring person you've ever heard – perhaps a really dull teacher you remember from school. For example, if you're saying, 'I'm not safe,' how would that sound in that most boring voice? Now, make the voice whiny. Then make it high pitched and squeaky, as if a chipmunk or Mickey Mouse was giving you the narration.

What happens when you play with the voice that way? How does it feel different?

As you altered the quality of the sound, notice how much less power it had. You may have found that the feelings became weaker or even insignificant. Indeed, it can almost be laughable so you can't take that voice seriously the next time you get scared.

▶ Posture ◀

Posture has been shown to affect a person's psychological wellbeing, both in terms of their sense of confidence and their self-esteem.

Try this simple experiment.

Focus for a moment on the thing that makes you scared, fearful or anxious.

As you focus on it, notice what happens to your body:

▶ Where do your eyes go?

▶ What happens to your breathing?

▶ To your shoulders?

▶ Where is your head?

Shake it out.

Now stick your chest right out, put your head back and your arms down but out to the sides and put the biggest smile you can manage on your face. While you are doing that, without moving a single muscle try to focus on that thing you are scared or phobic of.

In this position, you'll find it very difficult to focus on the object of your fears. Why? Because this physiology, this way of holding your body, is incompatible with fear. Which means that the secret to feeling good is surprisingly simple: all you need to do is change your body language – change how you're moving.

When you have a strong belief about something – for example that spiders, heights and thunder are dangerous – you act as though it's true, and more importantly, your body reacts like it is true, even though it isn't.

Remember the amygdala? If you believe you're in danger, your brain will trigger the fight, flight or freeze response: you break out into a cold sweat, your heart starts to race, you begin to breathe faster, and of course you may feel an urgent need to go to the loo.

So, now you're not just thinking about your fear, you're feeling afraid and your body is acting as though you're in real danger. Then, the rest of your body goes along with it. Some people try to curl up defensively, others grip their seat so hard their knuckles turn white.

You unconsciously think, 'Those are my danger signals. I must be in danger!' and the whole thing spirals. If having the physiology of fear is a signal to your brain to be afraid, it means we can start to break that spiral in a very simple way: simply by adopting a calm, relaxed physiology.

As we've seen, when we're scared or anxious our bodies often adopt defensive postures – and this is where our response to fear can spiral. Researchers have found that we can break this cycle, however, increasing feelings of power and risk tolerance and decreasing stress hormone levels by changing our posture. The change can turn off the preparation signals and disarm your amygdala. Adopting expansive postures (called power poses) can foster feelings of openness and assurance. A 2015 Harvard study by Amy Cuddy found that individuals who changed their posture before a high-stakes social evaluation felt more powerful and performed better. An open, confident and expansive posture makes it difficult to maintain the fearful focus, demonstrating the influence of our body language on our emotional state.

So next time you feel that fear, open up your body language, uncross your legs, sit back as though you're on the beach about to sunbathe and open your hands as though you're about to do yoga – your mind will follow suit and relax.

▶ Triggers ◀

Next, it's time to think about what triggers your anxiety, fear or phobia. Not the big picture but the details of specific situations. Just like the bell that made Pavlov's dogs salivate, all kinds of things can trigger the fear response in your mind. For you, it might be a particular sight, smell or sound, as in the following examples:

Fear of flying: the sound of the seatbelt sign coming on.

White-coat syndrome: the smell of the hospital.

Claustrophobia: the sight of people coming towards you.

Fear of dogs: hearing a dog bark or seeing a dog approaching.

And so on.

While stimulus responses are often set up accidentally or subconsciously, we can also artificially create our own to foster positive feelings such as excitement, enthusiasm and happiness.

To do this, we take intentional steps to get ourselves into that positive state and anchor it. The idea behind anchoring is that if you do something very exciting, relaxing or joyous and you perform a unique action at the moment when that feeling is at its peak, then in future whenever you perform that action again, you'll be back in that peak state. The action could be something like pulling your earlobe or touching your finger and forefinger together or making a fist with your hand. So, let's create our own stimulus response to feel good.

Start by recalling a time when you felt calm, centred and at peace (if you cannot think of a specific time, imagine what it would be like to feel this way).

Notice what was going on around you: what you were seeing, hearing and saying to yourself and any smells or tastes that went with it. Notice how you were breathing and how you were sitting or standing.

Allow yourself to fully re-experience those feelings of calm and peace, and when the feelings are at their peak, squeeze your fist tightly, hold it, and release it just as the feelings start to fade.

Stand up and shake off the feeling.

Next, recall another time when you couldn't stop laughing – perhaps you'd seen your favourite comedian telling a hilarious joke, or maybe something funny had just happened. Once again, notice what was going on around you: what you were seeing, hearing, saying to yourself and any smells or tastes that went with it. Notice how you were breathing and how you were sitting or standing.

If you find yourself laughing now, go with it. Allow yourself to laugh just as you did back then and, once again, as the feeling approaches its peak, squeeze your hand tightly into a fist, hold it, and release it as the emotion starts to fade.

Stand up and shake off the feeling.

Now, remember a time when you felt genuinely cared for and nurtured. Go back to that time and notice how you felt, what you were seeing, hearing and saying to yourself and any smells or tastes that went with it. Notice how you were breathing and how you were sitting or standing.

Once again, as the feeling approaches its peak, squeeze your hand tightly into a fist, hold it, and release it as the emotion starts to fade.

Stand up and shake off the feeling.

Finally, remember a time when you felt totally connected to someone or something: it could be a loved one, a friend, a pet or something else. What matters is the feeling of total connection. Go back to that time and notice how you felt, what you were seeing, hearing and saying to yourself and any smells or tastes that went with it. Notice how you were breathing and how you were sitting or standing.

Once again, as the feeling approaches its peak, squeeze your hand tightly into a fist, hold it, and release it as the emotion starts to fade.

Stand up and shake off the feeling.

It's worth noting that you can add more states to the same anchor, and you can use any states you want. But for now you've just set up an anchor with four positive states, so let's test it.

Without thinking of anything in particular, squeeze your fist together just like you did before. This time, you may notice that you start to feel calm, loved and connected, and you may also notice that you feel like laughing. That's your anchor being triggered.

► Feelings ◄

All these processes are ultimately designed to change how we feel about our phobia, and therefore how our mind and body react to it.

Emotions like fear create physical sensations within your body – butterflies, chills or heat, for example – that literally tell you that you're *feeling* fear. So, let's start by identifying what your fear feels like to you.

Ask yourself:

▻ What do I feel when I'm fearful?

▻ Where do I feel it?

▻ How intense is it?

Changing your feelings: Part 1

I got a call from a successful actor who told me she was about to go into an audition, and she was feeling afraid. The fear had come on very fast, and now she was outside the audition room and wanted to know what she could do to stop feeling this way. Short on time, I guided her through the same process that I'll share with you in a moment.

When we finished the process, she was underwhelmed, and she

said something along the lines of, 'Is that it?' However, when I told her to try to find the fear she had felt just ten seconds before, she was shocked to find she couldn't.

Afterwards, she told me it was the best she had felt at an audition, and she went on to get the role. The process goes like this:

1. Focus on the feeling that comes up when you think about your fear. Become aware of how the feeling moves around your body. Does it move clockwise or anticlockwise?

2. Now focus on the feeling. Take the feeling out of your body and spin it in front of you like a wheel. Follow the movement with your hand.

3. Notice if that feeling has a colour. Become aware of the colour, then change it to something more pleasing – bright white is often a good colour to change it to.

4. Now reverse the direction of the spin, and again, follow it with your hand.

5. Pull the feeling back into the body, still spinning it in the opposite direction.

6. Spin it faster and faster until it disappears.

Changing your feelings: Part 2

Research has shown the importance of tactile interactions, such as hugging, for our wellbeing.

One study from the University of Florida found that just twenty seconds of hugging was enough to dramatically reduce stress and anxiety. As Virginia Satir, a pioneer in family therapy, famously said: 'We need four hugs a day for survival. We need eight hugs a day for maintenance. We need twelve hugs a day for growth.'

Hugs release:

▶ Oxytocin, which plays a significant role in social bonding and feelings of trust, promoting a sense of connection, reducing stress and enhancing feelings of wellbeing.

▶ Serotonin, which is known to promote feelings of happiness, relaxation and contentment.

▶ Dopamine associated with pleasure and reward.

▶ Endorphins, which are natural pain-relieving and mood-enhancing chemicals.

So, with hugs and touch being so powerful at changing how we feel, do we need to find someone to hug every time we feel fearful? Well, here's the good news: the same chemicals can be released from hugging yourself. Try this:

1. Close your eyes and think about your phobia. What comes up for you and how strong is the feeling?

2. Cross your arms and put one hand on each shoulder, tap alternatively on each shoulder with your arms crossed. Do this for a few minutes.

3. Now move your hands all the way down your arms to your fingers, and then back up again.

4. Slowly stroke your cheeks with the back of your hands. Do this for a few minutes. Where is the feeling now?

Repeat as needed.

Using this self-soothing mechanism while focusing on your fear will often take out the emotional charge.

Putting it all together

As we talked about in Step 1, how would you teach someone the recipe for your phobia? What would you teach them? There is a strategy or recipe for everything we do in our lives, and as we've seen, there is also a set of ingredients (thoughts, feelings, how you breathe and move and what you see) that come together to cause you to be afraid – and you can also disrupt this pattern.

When you meet someone who doesn't have your fear, don't just say to them, 'Oh, you're so lucky.' Instead, ask them what they do in their head when they think about that same thing that you are fearful of: what do they think about, what do they feel, what images do they make in their head and what beliefs do they have about that thing?

Modelling someone without your phobia can be a powerful method for conquering our own fears. By observing individuals who remain fearless in the face of what frightens us, we can tap into their mindset and internal processes. This process involves what's called mirror neurons, which allow us to mimic their emotional responses and adopt their strategies for dealing with fear. Finding out their recipe and learning it is another way to achieve the overall aim of this step: rewiring our own brains and creating new associations.

STEP 4: QUICK RECAP

▷ Our fears and phobias can be compared to a recipe – changing any ingredient or submodality can alter the outcome.

▷ Our internal visualization and auditory and sensory experiences significantly contribute to the creation and magnification of our fears and phobias.

▷ Using humour or absurdity to picture our fears can reduce their impact on us.

▶ Questioning beliefs that instigate fear or hinder progress can uncover subconscious beliefs fuelling our fears or negative feelings.

▶ Techniques like reframing and moving our eyes can change the intensity associated with fears and beliefs.

▶ Creating a physical anchor, like squeezing your hand into a fist, can help in invoking positive feelings and shifting your emotional state.

STEP 5:
RELEASE THE PAST

So far, we've been working on rewriting the movie that you run in your head when you're scared. But, of course, to create these images, thoughts, feelings and beliefs about your phobia, there usually has to be something in your past that triggers this behaviour in the first place.

For the process in this section, we are going to look back to the history of our phobia we covered in Step I. As we saw earlier, there can be a direct or indirect link from the event to your phobia. In Step 5, we're going to go back and work on your memories of the event that first created your phobia: the time when you first learned to be afraid of it.

We've already seen that very often when we are fearful, we make big, bright pictures in our mind that end up making us even more frightened. We've also seen that if we change the images associated with the fear – make them black and white, move them about, make them funny etc. – we change the underlying feelings and take out the negative emotional charge. Now let's apply that to the trigger for your phobia.

Scrambling past memories

Neuroimaging has shown that the first time you see something new – a breathtaking landscape, a piece of art or even a complex equation – your brain's visual cortex, the part that processes visual information, springs into action. It's like a conductor leading an orchestra, coordinating a symphony of neural activity. Over time, as you become familiar with the sight, the conductor quiets down and the symphony fades to a gentle hum. This is a natural process called habituation.

But what happens when the sight is something scary, like a traumatic event or a phobia? Each time you recall that memory, your visual cortex conducts the same intense symphony as if you're experiencing the event for the very first time. It's as if your brain is stuck in a loop, replaying the same scary movie. The bigger the trauma, the stronger the visual recall becomes. This is why some people with PTSD suffer from constant flashbacks.

If we disrupt these visual memories with processes that scramble the images and disrupt the looping movie, we can change how we feel about our fears. These tools are sometimes called the Fast Phobia Model, Visual/Kinesthetic Dissociation (VKD) or the Rewind Process. They work by 'rewinding' and 'fast-forwarding' the phobic memory. Research has found these methods to be very effective with phobias.

Research by Shona Adams and Steven Allan, published in 2020, found that nearly half of the participants achieved full recovery by running this process just one to three times.

One theory on why scrambling visual memories changes phobias is that it disrupts the visual cortex's storage of the fearful event, creating rapid habituation and thus disconnecting the memory from the emotion.

Fast phobia/rewind

1. Imagine you are sitting in a cinema looking at a blank screen. Make the cinema look just perfect for you and imagine that the seat is the comfiest you have ever sat in.

2. When you're happy with the theatre and your seat, imagine floating up out of your body and into the projection booth, high above all the seats in the cinema so that you can look back and see yourself calmly sitting in the cinema looking at the screen.

3. When was the very first time you created your phobia? What was the very first event? In your own time, let your mind wander back – and if you cannot remember that very first time, focus on a significant event that you do remember. Notice the feelings that come up as you think about the event. On a scale of 0 to 10 (0 being not at all, 10 being the highest), how strong is the feeling?

4. In a moment, a black-and-white movie is going to play on the screen. When that happens, I don't want you to watch the screen. Instead, you're going to look back down from the projection booth to where you are sitting in the theatre and just watch yourself sitting there calmly in the cinema, watching the screen that is playing the movie.

5. The movie that is going to play on the screen is of the time when you first felt that fear, from the moment just before the event happened through to the moment afterwards when you were safe.

6. When you're ready, watch yourself as the movie starts to play in black and white. Remember: look back down from the projection booth to where you are sitting in the theatre and just watch yourself sitting there calmly in the cinema, watching the screen that is playing the movie.

7. When the movie comes to an end and you're safe again, white-out the screen.

8. Float back down into your seat from the projection booth and then float out of your seat and into the screen so that you put yourself inside the movie.

9. Once you're there, run the film at high speed backwards in colour from the end – the time when you were safe after the event – back to the beginning before it all happened, where again the was no fear.

10. When you get back to the beginning of the movie, white-out the screen once more.

11. Float back out of the screen, down into your seat and then back up into the projection booth.

12. Again, look down from the elevated projection booth to where you are seated calmly watching the phobic event play out on the screen as you run the movie forwards in black and white to the end. When it's finished, white-out the screen.

Repeat steps 9 to 12, making sure to speed up the backwards movie in step 9. Make it run backwards at five-times normal speed, and as you do, add comedy music and images. Could you add some furry animal ears? Could you add a fast, squeaky voice? Could you add other people or things to the situation to make it even more comical? Could you change the speed so that everyone is moving comically fast, like an old silent movie?

When the emotion of the phobia has lessened, imagine floating up above the whole thing and ask yourself: 'What learning can I take from this event that will help me in future?'

Some people are able to do this process just once and get instant results. For others, it takes a little getting used to – there's a lot to do setting up the cinema screen and playing through the scenario, so practise the steps until you get the hang of the technique.

Do the time warp

Einstein's theory of relativity states that there is no absolute frame of reference to time and that the perception of an event can be different depending on the observer's point of view.

Have you ever noticed how time seems to be so slow when you're stuck doing a boring job? Every second can feel like an eternity. On the other hand, when you're having a blast and enjoying yourself, time flies by in the blink of an eye. And if you forget the next line of your speech? Suddenly, twenty seconds feel like they stretch on forever, especially if you have a fear of public speaking. And if you drop something breakable, like a priceless piece of glass, everything seems to go into slow motion.

We store time in our minds in one of two ways: temporal and atemporal. Temporal storage refers to the chronological storage of events, where each event is situated along a linear timeline, similar to the way we perceive the progression of time. In other words, we remember events in the order in which they occurred. This is how we typically understand our memories, moving from past to present and anticipating the future.

Atemporal storage, on the other hand, refers to a non-linear, non-chronological way of storing experiences. Instead of being associated with a specific point in time, memories and emotions are stored in a more associative manner. In this form of storage, one memory could trigger another regardless of when it happened in time. It is more about the emotional connection between experiences than their temporal sequence.

For example, the scent of a certain perfume might evoke a number of memories and emotions, irrespective of the chronological order in which those memories occurred.

We can use our understanding of our mind's temporal storage to work with emotional events that created our phobia using what's called our timeline. We're not consciously aware of those lines, but we can bring them into our awareness. The use of these types of tools has been shown to be effective, with a 2022 study at the University of Lahore finding that timeline tools helped a significant majority of participants in changing their fears.

Before we look to change our phobia, first let's find our timeline with a simple exercise.

It's a closed-eye process, so you'll need to read through the instructions several times and memorize the steps.

1. Close your eyes and think back to your twenty-first birthday.

2. As you think about that memory, you'll notice that it's located somewhere in space. You might be aware of the memory being in front of you, behind you or to one side, or it may even be inside you. Also, notice where it is vertically: is it above you, below you or on the same level?

3. Once you've located that memory of your twenty-first birthday, think about your sixteenth birthday and notice where it is located.

4. If you didn't notice it before, notice now the relationship between the two memories and where they are stored.

5. Next, whatever age you are now, think about your last birthday and notice how that is stored in your mind.

6. If you focus on those three memories, could they describe a line? It might be a straight line, or it might be a curve, but if you put them in order – your sixteenth birthday, your twenty-first birthday and your last birthday – you'll notice they are on a line.

7. Now, if you know where the line is for your past, you can
    also work out where the line is that stretches out into
    your future. So, do that now. Imagine an event you know is
    coming up in the next week – maybe a meeting or a meal
    with friends. Notice where it is. Then imagine an event a
    month from now, and then one a year from now. Each time,
    do the same as you did for the past and notice the line for
    your future.

Once you've identified where your timeline is, you can open your
eyes and come back to full awareness.

Temporal reprocessing method

Our minds often lean on the past, especially our early years. All
too often these early years guide our decision-making and these
beliefs continue to rule our decisions in the present day.

But think about it: would you take life advice from a ten-
year-old? Likely not. Yet many of our choices, particularly those
related to our phobias, are based on decisions and emotions
we formed long ago, often even before we had a comprehensive
understanding of the world. So, we need to change those
outdated beliefs and emotions from our past. And while our past
can teach us valuable lessons, it shouldn't dictate our future.

Our perception of past events is subjective and can be changed.
We have the ability to 'travel' back to these moments and modify
our perspective, influencing the emotional impact they have on
us in the present, just as Einstein's theory of relativity says our
perception of time can be flexible and altered.

As we saw earlier in the book, your fear was created by a
significant event in your past – you can think of it as the trigger or
seed for your phobia. There may be multiple significant events in
your past related to your fear, but there will be one, way back, that
started it all. And, because of the way your mind stores memories,

if we can clear that event from your timeline, it will cause the others to fall away too. So, unlike most of the other tools we have covered. This process doesn't just change one event but has a generative effect, changing multiple fearful memories in one go.

To clear the event, we are going to float above our timeline and travel back to that very first event as observers so that we can take positive lessons, learnings and insights from it. Then we will come back along the timeline to the present, learning from and clearing all the similar events that have happened since then. And because our mind is the only thing capable of travelling faster than the speed of light, we can do all of that in minutes rather than decades.

Why does this approach work? It taps into an incredible brain ability called neuroplasticity. This means our brains can rewire themselves, forming new connections based on our thoughts and emotions. In this process, we leverage this feature to re-associate past events with more positive emotions.

Another essential aspect is memory reconsolidation. Each time we remember something, it's not set in stone. We have the power to modify it before recalling it again. We can actively change how we recall challenging memories, transforming them to feel more neutral or even positive. Furthermore, it essentially allows an emotional release. It provides a safe space for us to express and let go of pent-up emotions tied to past events, offering a sort of spring clean for the mind. Overall, this approach helps us revisit, reframe and release negative emotions or limiting beliefs tied to past events.

Removing the charge from the root event

Let's find the root of your phobia. Ask yourself, 'When was the very first time I felt this emotion? How old was I?' Let an age come into your head. Trust the answer that comes up, even if you don't know what it is. The connection between the event and your phobia might not be directly obvious, but it's most likely going to be before you were aged eight.

If nothing shows up, do the process anyway and the answer might become clear as you do.

Step I: Imagine your life is a line on the floor, following the shape you discovered above. Stand at the point on this line that represents now, and walk backwards along the line until you reach the age you identified above (you may feel a pull in your body when you're in the right place).

Step 2: Stepping off the line, move away as far as you need to in order not to feel any negative emotions about the event and watch from a distance.

Step 3: Ask yourself, 'On a scale of I to I0, how strong are the emotions in this event?'

Step 4: As you watch your younger self, what can the older you teach the younger you to help let go of that fear?

Step 5: If you could have brought a mentor or guide to that event, what advice would they give you to help you look at the situation differently?

Step 6: Take five deep breaths, step back into the event, dart your eyes left and right ten times, then step out of the event and watch the event from a distance again.

Step 7: Imagine a colour of relaxation and beam it into the event so it fills the whole event and floods it with light.

Step 8: Imagine stepping back from the event further back in time and watching it before it ever happened. On a scale from 0 to 10, how strong are the emotions now? If the emotions are at 0, move to step 9. If not, repeat steps 2 to 8 again.

If you find you are still having trouble getting to 0, it may be that this is not the first event. Try walking back further.

Step 9: Once the emotions are at 0, start slowly walking forward from this first event to the present, noticing all the other events through your life where you had these similar emotions.

Step 10: When you find one of these later events, repeat steps 2-8 for each event until you get back to now.

Done right, this process should feel like a 'defrag' for your mind and can leave you feeling either extremely energized or relaxed.

STEP 5: QUICK RECAP

This step looked at releasing the past through various techniques.

▶ The methods explored in this section help to release past fears and alter our perception of phobias.

▶ Our brains can habituate fear, playing a 'scary movie' repeatedly.

▶ Disrupting this fear loop through methods like the fast phobia model and the rewind process helps to modify our visual associations with the phobia. Guided through a visualization exercise in a cinema scenario to show this.

▶ An understanding of temporal storage can be used to work with the emotional events creating our phobia through a mental timeline. Guided through how to identify the root event that caused our phobia, often a moment in childhood before the age of eight.

▶ It is important to revisit, reframe and release negative emotions or limiting beliefs tied to the root event.

STEP 6:
RECONDITION YOUR EMOTIONS

By now you have seen the importance of the movies and imagery that you are putting into your mind. For example, there aren't many runners who like to get up at 5 a.m. on a cold morning to go and train. Imagine if when the alarm went off, they just lay in the dark thinking about what it was going to be like running in the cold and the wet, seeing themselves shivering and miserable. The chances are they would turn off the alarm, roll over in their nice, warm bed and go back to sleep. And they wouldn't win many races.

So, what do professional athletes or anybody who is willing to face things they don't like think about instead? They focus on success. They see themselves on the podium with the gold medal around their neck. They hear the cheers of the crowd. That makes it a lot easier to get out of bed and train.

When it comes to facing your phobia, then, what are you thinking about? What would happen if rather than seeing yourself panicking, you instead focused on the reason you wanted to get over it – for example, the round of applause from your speech, the joy of travelling, seeing wildlife, being at peace, living your life freely or just be more relaxed in your body? It's all about focus.

Switching the imagery

Ask yourself: 'What am I actually focusing on when I think about my phobia? What am I putting in my mind to make myself feel bad?' If you were to change that, how would you feel?

With that in mind, when you think about your phobia, what mental images would you like to see in your mind instead? What would you like to imagine? In this exercise, you're going to switch the imagery in your head, from the negative, fear-inducing pictures you have been giving yourself to something more positive and enticing.

1. **Identify the phobia:** Identify what you're afraid of. For instance, if it's spiders, the moment you see a spider may trigger an intense fear response.

2. **Create a trigger image:** Close your eyes and visualize a situation where you encounter your phobia. This could be the thing you are afraid of suddenly appearing in your visual field. Make this image as clear and detailed as possible. This image should be from your point of view, as if you're experiencing it in real-time.

3. **Create a desired image:** Now, visualize yourself in the future, confidently dealing with the situation that used to trigger your phobia. Imagine yourself seeing the thing you are scared of and remaining calm and unafraid. This image should be compelling and full of positive emotion. However, see this image as if you're looking at yourself from the outside, as if it's a picture of yourself on a movie screen.

4. **Now you have two images:** The trigger image and the desired image. See the trigger image in great detail. Then,

picture a small, dark, desired image at the bottom corner of the trigger image. The desired image represents the new response you want to have in the presence of the phobia.

5. **Replace the trigger image:** In your mind, have the desired image quickly grow in size and brightness while the trigger image becomes smaller and darker until it is completely replaced by the desired image. Make this change as quickly and energetically as you can.

6. **Blank your mind:** Open your eyes, move around or do something to distract yourself and 'clear' your mental screen.

7. **Repeat:** Repeat steps 4–6 around five to seven times, or until when you think about the trigger image, the desired image naturally and automatically comes to mind.
   Each time you repeat the exercise, you may notice the old image is harder to bring up, or dimmer or less sharp. Keep repeating it until you find it hard to find the old negative images and feelings. When all that's left is the new, positive imagery, notice what you feel and see.

EXAMPLES OF PHOBIAS YOU CAN SWITCH:

▶ **Fear of flying (aviophobia):** For your trigger image, visualize yourself getting anxious as you're about to board a plane. For your desired image, picture yourself calmly settling into your seat, looking out the window and enjoying the flight.

▶ **Fear of heights (acrophobia):** The trigger image could be you standing at the edge of a high balcony, feeling your heart race. The desired image is you standing at the same spot, calmly enjoying the view.

▶ **Fear of public speaking (glossophobia):** For the trigger image, imagine the moment just before you step onto a stage, feeling panic and dread. Your desired image could be you delivering your speech confidently and clearly and receiving a round of applause.

▶ **Fear of dogs (cynophobia):** Visualize a dog approaching you as your trigger image, bringing feelings of fear. For the desired image, see yourself petting a dog calmly and enjoying the interaction.

The key to success with this exercise is repetition and emotional intensity. It may take some time to notice changes, but keep practising. Your subconscious mind will start to associate the old trigger with the new, more empowering response.

Tapping yourself free

There are a number of therapies that are based on the idea of tapping, including emotional freedom technique, thought field therapy and meridian tapping. These work by tapping on different points of your body while focusing on your fear.

There are a number of different theories as to why it works, though the original developers linked it to meridians from eastern medicine, similar to acupuncture. Other people have suggested it works by bilateral stimulation in a similar way to the eye movements explored in Step 4.

But while people may disagree on why it works, most people agree that it does. A number of research studies have shown the effectiveness of tapping techniques in treating phobias. Patrice Rancour's 2017 study, titled 'The Emotional Freedom Technique', took sixty research articles in peer-reviewed journals and reported a staggering 98 per cent efficacy rate in tapping as a treatment for psychological distress. With that in mind, let's move on to the next exercise.

Focus on your phobia – what emotions come up?

Rate that emotion out of 10 (0 = no fear; 10 = the most fearful)

Hand: Take two fingers of one hand and tap on the side of the other hand, on the part you would use if you were going to chop wood karate-style.

Say what you fear out loud and keep repeating it as you do the following.

Fingers: Tap each finger on either side of the nail.
Eyebrow: Tap just above and to one side of your nose, at the beginning of the eyebrow.
Side of the eye: Tap on the bone bordering the outside corner of each eye.
Under the eye: Tap on the bone under each eye below the pupil.
Under the nose: Tap on the indentation between the bottom of your nose and the top of your upper lip.
Chin: Tap midway between the point of your chin and the bottom of your lower lip.
Collarbone: Tap on the junction where the sternum (breastbone), collarbone and the first rib meet.
Under the arm: Tap on the side of the body, about 4 inches below the armpit.
Top of the head: Hold your fingers together back-to-back and tap all over the top of your head.

Finally, say that belief out loud again. Out of ten, how strong is the emotion now?

Now, what normally happens is that as you go through the exercise, the emotional impact reduces. Sometimes, the feelings lessen and something else comes up. If your mind has wandered to another event, whether you know why or not, it's probably significant.

Repeat the process until the fear feels unimportant.

After the last tap, take a deep breath in and shake off any feelings that remain. Repeat as needed.

Anchoring facing your fear

Visualization techniques like we are doing have been shown to alter the physical structure and function of our brain, reinforcing the connections between neurons in ways that help to improve motor control, confidence and motivation.

It's all very well making yourself feel good for a moment by thinking positively, but how do you make sure those good feelings stay so you can access them whenever you want? In this process, which is similar to the one we used in Step 4, you'll create a positive anchor associated with great experiences of facing your fear, so you can carry this positive feeling with you any time you need it.

I. **Choose a space:** Find a quiet, comfortable place where you can move around a little. Imagine a circle on the floor around you.

2. **Identify desired state:** Think about how you'd like to feel when you come face-to-face with your phobia. This might be calm, confident, unafraid etc.

3. **Recall a past experience:** Recall a time when you felt this desired state strongly. It doesn't have to be related to the phobia. It might be a time you felt particularly confident,

calm or in control. Immerse yourself in this memory. What do you see, hear and feel? Amplify these sensations and emotions until they are very strong.

4. **Step into the circle:** As you're feeling this powerful state, step into your circle. Anchor this feeling to the circle. Imagine the circle glowing with a colour that represents this state. Spend some time experiencing this state in the circle.

5. **Step out of the circle:** When you're ready, step out of the circle, leaving the powerful feelings within it.

6. **Test the circle:** Shake off the state, move around a little and clear your mind. Then, step back into the circle. You should feel the desired state return. If it doesn't, repeat steps 3 to 5.

7. **Link to music:** Now, add in a piece of motivational music that uplifts you and resonates with the state you want to embody as you step into the circle.

8. **Add in support:** Imagine a person you admire for their courage or calmness in the face of adversity. Visualize them with you, offering advice and support as you face your phobia.

9. **Shrink the circle:** Now, visualize a miniaturized version of your circle in the palm of your hand. This represents your ability to access this powerful state wherever and whenever you need it.

10. **Face the phobia now:** Visualize a future situation where you will encounter your phobia. As you visualize this situation, step into your circle. Feel the confidence, calm or control fill you up as you face your fear in your visualization.

Congratulations! You've just created a positive anchor. Notice how you feel differently.

STEP 6: QUICK RECAP

▶ The power of perspective is vital in managing phobias – there is a need to focus on successful outcomes rather than fearful ones.

▶ Vivid trigger images can induce fear, but we can also form a desired image of ourselves confidently addressing the fear. We can then gradually replace the trigger image with the desired image until the latter automatically comes to mind.

▶ Techniques to 'anchor' these positive states can be invoked when encountering the phobia in the future, enabling a more empowered response.

STEP 7:
REALIZE A POWERFUL FUTURE

A wise man once saw a woman weeping by the riverside. He asked what ailed her. Through her tears, she shared her fears about what may happen to her children in the future – sickness, heartbreak, poverty. The man listened quietly and then asked, 'Are these troubles occurring now?'

'No,' she admitted, 'but they could happen tomorrow.'

He gently said, 'Then you are borrowing trouble from tomorrow and letting it steal your peace today. Attend to the present and let tomorrow care for itself.'

As we have seen, fear is not something you catch like a cold. It's something you do to yourself, albeit subconsciously with your thoughts, your beliefs, your feelings, your imagination and your emotions.

For instance, let's say you feel great right now, but then you think, 'What if I don't feel like this in a week?' In order for you to feel good right now and then not feel good in a week's time, you would have to change something: the pictures you make inside your mind, your thoughts, your feelings and your internal dialogue. In other words, you'd have to follow an emotional recipe, as we discussed in Step 4.

Of course, once you become aware of your negative patterns, you can start targeting and changing them. So, if you notice yourself making a negative mental movie, you can immediately begin to change it, as we've seen in the previous steps: running it backwards, playing with the soundtrack, making it black and white, pushing it out into the distance etc.

Does thinking about your phobia help? Well, as we saw earlier it does not, but often when people live in the future, worrying, focusing on the what-ifs and yeah, buts, they are harbouring a belief that if they mentally rehearse danger, it will somehow prepare them to face it if it arises. There's a big problem with that approach: while you're running through that worst-case scenario, your brain doesn't know the difference between what is imagined and what is real. So, every time you imagine the worst-case scenario, you trigger your fear reflex and your body releases adrenaline and other hormones, and you end up feeling as bad as if it was actually happening. That would be fine if it got you ready to face danger. But, as we've already seen, that is far from the case. All those negative thoughts, images, self-talk and everything else simply reinforces the problem.

Now, it's hard to deal with danger when you're crippled by fear. So, the next time you find yourself thinking, 'I need to be ready for this,' imagine yourself completely relaxed, calm, centred and ready. What would that do to your stress levels? How much better would you feel?

Creating a positive belief in the future
We said earlier that if you try to resist your fear, it will just push back harder. Since you can't deal with the phobia by resisting

it, what can you do instead? You have to create new positive associations and use them to replace your fear of the future.

There's a phrase I hear all the time from my clients: 'What if?' What if I let go of this fear and I'm not safe? What if? What if? What if? People can run these what-ifs hundreds of times a day, for every possible scenario, especially when they are suffering from extreme anxiety. If you have a phobia, it tends to come up as you get closer to a trigger event. For example, as the day of your doctor's appointment, big speech or plane journey gets closer, you may start to wonder, 'What if this happens or I do this?', 'What if somebody does that?', 'What if I panic?' and so on. These types of thoughts are especially common when your fear is linked to anxiety.

In this section, we are going to work on those what-ifs and the recurring thoughts that prompt them.

Often, we are so used to dismissing the recurring thoughts that go with what-ifs as 'silly' or 'illogical' that we fail to even acknowledge them, but we need to bring them into our conscious awareness in order to challenge them and let them go.

Think about any of the what-ifs or yeah, buts you may have about facing your fear. For example: 'What if I'm not safe?' Or, 'I feel OK now, but what if I feel bad later' and so on? Write all the what-ifs down on paper, look at the first statement you wrote down and ask yourself: 'From 0 to 10, how likely is this really to happen?'

Now rate the intensity of the emotion that goes with them and put them in order from strongest to weakest. When you've rated each statement, say it out loud and notice any feelings and emotions that go with it.

Now, we're going to go through the list one by one and challenge each thought. We'll be using the tapping techniques you learned in Step 4, but instead of focusing on the past we are going to focus on fear of the future, the what-ifs.

Repeat the what-ifs out loud and go through the tapping sequence.

Step I: Focus on the what-if thoughts and beliefs you wrote down and start to say them out loud, loudly and in a clear, confident voice.

Step 2: Next, use the tapping technique you learned earlier. Repeating the what-if out loud over and over again, do the following:

Hand: Take two fingers of one hand and tap on the side of the other hand, on the part you would use if you were going to chop wood karate-style.

Fingers: Tap each finger on either side of the nail.

Eyebrow: Tap just above and to one side of your nose, at the beginning of the eyebrow.

Side of the eye: Tap on the bone bordering the outside corner of each eye.

Under the eye: Tap on the bone under each eye, about I inch below the pupil.

Under the nose: Tap on the indentation between the bottom of your nose and the top of your upper lip.

Chin: Tap midway between the point of your chin and the bottom of your lower lip.

Collarbone: Tap on the junction where the sternum (breastbone), collarbone and the first rib meet.

Under the arm: Tap on the side of the body, about 4 inches below the armpit.

Top of the head: Hold your fingers together back-to-back and tap all around the top of your skull.

When you're ready, repeat the process with the second item on the list, then the third and so on, until you run out of what-ifs. As you keep repeating the what-ifs and tapping, you should find that the emotions attached to it get weaker.

Most people spend their time focusing on what-ifs that never happen. So why not focus on what-ifs that make you smile, feel joyful and are fun, even if they seem unlikely. Make a list of the positive things you'd like to say to yourself the next time you face your fear, such as the positive what-ifs and beliefs that you'd like to have. Rate them from 0 to 100 per cent on how true they feel.

Now repeat the tapping exercise above, focusing on the positive what-ifs instead. After each round of tapping, check-in on your positive what-if and notice if it feels more true. Keep tapping until it's at a percentage you are happy with, then move on to another positive thought.

Sometimes you may feel some resistance, and your inner voice and thought starts to focus on disempowering what-ifs again. Don't worry if this happens; it just means there might be a few other unhelpful beliefs and thoughts still left. If so, just loop back and focus on the negative what-if process and tap on them.

Turning down the anticipation dial

Another great method to deal with fear of the future and to ground yourself is turning down the anticipation dial. The following exercise is a tool to help manage these feelings of apprehension.

1. **Relax your body:** Close your eyes and breathe deeply. Inhale deeply, filling your lungs with air and exhale slowly, releasing any tension. Do this several times until you start to feel your body relax.

2. **Progressive relaxation:** Begin at your toes and progress through your body. Contract each muscle group for a few seconds, then release it. Pay attention to the sensation of

relaxation in each muscle; this helps deepen your state of relaxation.

3. **Visualization of stress level:** Imagine a dial in your mind. This dial ranges from 0 to 10, where 10 represents the highest level of stress and 0 represents complete relaxation.

4. **Identify your current stress level:** Observe the dial. Which number is it on? This number represents your current stress level.

5. **Gradually decrease stress:** Imagine yourself slowly turning the dial down. As the dial decreases, envision your stress diminishing, your muscles relaxing further and your mind becoming increasingly calm.

6. **Slow and steady:** Take your time with this process. Reduce the dial gradually, pausing between each level to take a deep breath. With each reduction, remind yourself, 'I am becoming calmer and more relaxed.'

7. **Reach a comfortable stress level:** Continue this process until the dial is at a number that represents a comfortable level of stress for you.

8. **Visualize a new dial:** Now, imagine a second dial in your mind. This dial represents positive emotions like relaxation, peace, joy and happiness and also ranges from 0 to 10, where 10 is the highest intensity of positive emotions.

9. **Turning up positive emotions:** Visualize yourself slowly turning this dial up. As you do, envision the positive emotions growing stronger, filling your body and mind.

10. **Steady increase:** Again, take your time with this process. Increase the dial gradually, taking deep breaths between each level. As you turn the dial up, remind yourself: 'I am becoming more relaxed, peaceful and joyful.'

II. **Reach your desired level of positive emotions:** Continue until you reach a level that feels comfortable for you.

12. **Imprint the positive state:** Once you reach your desired level, allow yourself a few moments to enjoy this positive state. Visualize the positive emotions infusing every part of your body, rooting you in this peaceful state.

13. **Anchor the feeling:** Squeeze your fingers together and anchor this positive feeling.

14. **Return to the present:** When you feel ready, bring yourself back to the present and notice how you feel differently now!

The future feelings process

How would it feel to imagine the pleasure of overcoming your fear, phobia or anxiety before it ever happened? Anxiety is really nothing more than fear of the future; it's the anticipation of something bad happening 'later'. So, we can deal with it by replacing that negative future vision with a vision of something good.

In Step 5, I showed you how to go back into the past along your timeline and clear the negative events that created your phobia. In the same way, we can also travel forward along the timeline, into the future. For example, you can take yourself to a point in time after you've successfully faced your fear and imagine what it will be like when you're enjoying the moment. You drop down into that moment and notice how you feel. Now, when you focus on those feelings and that learning of how you'll feel after successfully facing your fear, you can let go of the anticipatory anxiety.

Step I: Stand at the point on your timeline that represents 'now' and walk forward along the line until you reach a point in the future where you anticipate facing your phobia.

Step 2: Step off the line and move away as far as you need. From a distance, watch this future self who is facing the situation successfully and with ease.

Step 3: Ask yourself, 'On a scale of I to 10, how strong are the positive emotions in this event?'

Step 4: Take five deep breaths, step into this future event, dart your eyes left and right ten times, then step out of the event and watch it from a distance again.

Step 5: Beam a colour of relaxation and success into the event, filling it with light.

Step 6: Imagine stepping back from the event further in the future and watching it before it ever happened. On a scale from 0 to 10, how strong are the positive emotions now? If the emotions are at 10, move to step 7. If not, repeat steps 2 to 6 again.

Step 7: Once the emotions are at 10, start slowly walking back from this future event to the present.

Step 8: As you walk back from the future to the present, notice every step and every change you made along the way to get to the place of successfully facing your fear.

Step 9: Notice how your perspective on your current fear or anxiety has shifted.

Heart breathing

The connection between the heart and the mind has long been talked about in romance novels, poems and moments of heartbreak.

Science now understands that the heart isn't just a pump moving blood around our bodies – it also offers us a powerful way to become centred and calm. Research from the HeartMath Institute has found that the heart and the brain are intricately connected in ways that go beyond mere metaphors and poetic expressions. The institute's research revealed that the heart sends more signals to the brain than the brain sends to the heart. These heart signals have a significant effect on brain function, influencing emotional processing as well as higher cognitive faculties, such as attention, perception, memory, problem-solving and, most importantly, our stress levels. The level of alignment between our heart and brain can be measured through what's called heart rate variability (HRV). This differs from standard heart rate monitoring as it measures the variations in the time intervals between heartbeats and their patterns, so rather than just tracking the overall heart rate, HRV can tell us our body's level of stress.

So how can we change our HRV? Heart breathing works by focusing on our breath and the rhythm of our heart. By doing this you can manage your stress response and create a more coherent HRV pattern.

1. Close your eyes and place your attention on your heart. Imagine you're breathing in and out from your heart, finding a rhythm that is slow and comfortable.

2. As you breathe, bring to mind something you are profoundly grateful for. Immerse yourself in this memory or feeling, engaging as many senses as you can.

3. As you inhale, imagine drawing feelings of gratitude into your heart.

4. On your exhale, visualize releasing stress, anxiety or any negative emotion.

5. Now, bring to mind a feeling of connection. This could be a connection with a loved one, with nature or with the universe. Visualize this connection as a colour that resonates with you.

6. Next, focus on feelings of safety and comfort. Imagine these feelings as a warm colour. As you breathe in, visualize this colour filling your body and heart, making you feel secure and protected.

7. With your exhale, release any feelings of fear or worry along with your breath.

8. Now focus on happiness. Recall a moment when you felt truly joyful and free. Visualize this happiness as a bright, vibrant colour.

9. Imagine this colour spreading from your head down to your heart as you inhale, filling your entire being with happiness. As you exhale, visualize any remaining tension leaving your body.

10. Continue this process for as long as it feels comfortable. With each breath, draw in more feelings of connection, safety and happiness and release any negativity.

11. Now imagine yourself facing your fear.

STEP 7: QUICK RECAP

▷ Anticipatory anxiety is essentially a fear of future events, often manifesting as excessive worry about what might happen.

▷ Visualization is a powerful tool in producing a successful outcome in future fear-inducing situations, helping to replace fear with positive anticipation.

▶ It is possible to learn to challenge and weaken the emotions attached to our what-if scenarios, helping us to reduce our fear about the future. Practised tapping on what-ifs.

▶ We can travel forward along our timeline to feel the pleasure of overcoming our fears before they happen.

▶ Heart breathing can be used for stress management, focusing on the heart's rhythm and using gratitude, connection, safety and happiness to manage stress and create a balanced HRV.

PART 3

Exploring the Most Common Phobias

THE THINGS THAT SCARE US

In Part I, we tackled the big question: what exactly is a phobia? Then, in Part 2, we got down to the business of changing our fears. Now, we're on to the grand finale of this book, where we'll shine a spotlight on the top ten phobias that get people's hearts racing, plus a handful of the weirdest and most unexpected ones out there.

We're going to walk through fears that come courtesy of Mother Nature herself, like lightning-lit storms and towering cliffs. We'll peek into the awkward world of social phobias like public speaking, where even a simple 'hello' can seem daunting, and we'll check out those situational scares, like the white-knuckle experience of being up in the air flying. And yes, we'll talk about the creepy-crawlies and spiders that send shivers down many people's spines. Ever wonder why some folks break out in a cold sweat at the sight of a clown, feel queasy when confronted by a slice of Swiss cheese or bolt at the sight of facial hair? We'll dive into that in our section on odd phobias.

As we dig into these fears, we'll unpack how culture, society, environment and even the latest TV show can make our phobias stick like superglue. We'll also bust some of the myths that keep us in a loop of fear and give you the facts that can help you change your beliefs about your phobia. If your phobia didn't make the list or doesn't slot neatly into these boxes, don't worry. Just find the chapter that feels closest to home. The good news? The tricks we covered in Part 2 are effective with any phobia.

As you read through this section, you might stumble upon other triggers or thoughts that you hadn't noticed before. That's great for when you circle back to the 'Seven Rs' from Part 2. So, let's start untangling these fears.

FEAR OF BUGS AND INSECTS

Insects have been on this planet for a long time. The earliest insects are believed to have been around 385 to 359 million years ago, and some estimates suggest there could be anywhere from 2.5 million to 30 million species in the world today. When it comes to a phobia of bugs, about 25 per cent of people are afraid of them, and 40 per cent of all phobias come under the banner of fear of insects. This used to be a big one for me too.

One summer night as a young child, I was tucked up in bed with the gentle glow of my night light dimly illuminating my room. I was sleeping when, unexpectedly and abruptly, I was disturbed by an intrusive, never-ending buzzing. I was instantly wide awake: my eyes shot open and I quickly surveyed the room. An intense wave of emotion overcame me as I saw a giant wasp circling, and I jumped out of bed and ran to the comfort and security of my parents' bedroom.

When I returned with my parents, my room had become eerily quiet. There was no trace of the wasp and no open doors or windows. They kindly admonished me and hinted at the possibility of me dreaming up the whole episode, and guided by their comforting assurance I returned to my bed and tried to go back to sleep.

Once again, the buzzing started, courtesy of that pesky wasp. In the faint glow, I saw it rising from behind my bedside lamp. I ran to get my mother again, but to my irritation and unease the wasp vanished again, and I began to feel this buzzing creature was deliberately toying with me.

Luckily, as my mother was about to dismiss my fear once more and leave the room, the wasp revealed itself – and finally I felt heard and understood. She quickly removed this flying menace; however, this moment was the initial trigger for a long-lasting fear of wasps, and other unpleasant incidents reinforced this fear as I grew up, making things worse.

When I started looking into this fear as an adult, I realized that my phobia of wasps wasn't just a result of the unsettling buzz or the threat of a painful sting; it was also the fear of not feeling heard and feeling isolated and alone. This secondary issue overlaid with my fear of wasps and shaped my interactions with them long into adulthood.

Wasps, bees and hornets are high on the list of most-common bug phobias; however, one bug trumps them. It's top of most phobia lists, and even though it's not technically a bug or an insect, it gets grouped in with them. It is, of course, the spider.

Fear of spiders (arachnophobia)

Spiders are fascinating creatures that have been around for millions of years. They are part of the arachnid family and can be found in almost every corner of the world. Spiders are known for their ability to spin silk webs, which they use to catch prey and create shelters.

Despite their many interesting traits, however, spiders are objects of fear for many people. Look at any list of the most common phobias and you'll likely find arachnophobia somewhere near the top. It affects millions of individuals worldwide. In fact, some studies have shown that more than 471 million people worldwide have a fear of spiders. This fear is often irrational, as the risk of harm coming from a spider is actually very low.

In comparison, other insects and bugs, such as mosquitoes, are much more dangerous. Mosquitoes are known to carry a number of deadly diseases, including malaria, dengue fever and Zika virus. They are responsible for killing approximately 1 million people worldwide each year. Despite this, while they are not often liked, very few people have an actual phobia of mosquitoes.

As with most phobias, the fear of spiders often has more to do with our associations and perceptions than any actual risks. Many famous individuals, including Justin Timberlake, Jennifer Lawrence, Miley Cyrus, Kim Kardashian, Taylor Swift and Gwyneth Paltrow, to name a few, have said they have a fear of spiders. Actor Rupert Grint, known for his role as Ron Weasley in the *Harry Potter* films, also has a lifelong fear of spiders, in a phobia he shares with his on-screen persona. This is perhaps unsurprising given that during the filming of *Harry Potter and the Chamber of Secrets* there was a scene that involved Grint's character coming face-to-face with giant spiders. Even though the spiders were mechanical props and animatronics, Grint had a visible adverse reaction. The mere sight of giant arachnids, realistic or not, triggered his real-life phobia. Years later, Grint has said that to this day he still struggles to watch the film due to his intense fear.

I myself have struggled with arachnophobia as well. I absolutely adored most animals as a child – wasps and large spiders being the few exceptions – but the large spider fear turned out to be a major issue for keeping a job. When I was in my teens, I saw a part-time job opportunity at a pet shop and applied without a second thought. However, upon arriving for my interview I found that this pet shop was the only one in the area that specialized in ... yep, you guessed it: tarantulas.

The owner quickly discovered my dislike of spiders. He found the situation quite amusing and decided to place a tarantula on my hand. Despite nearly being overcome by fear, I tried my hardest to keep my composure and hold the spider, nearly dropping it. After that, I soon realized that this job was not for me and walked away rather quickly.

Even being given a few basic facts about spiders might have helped to ease my mind. Even back then, I realized that simply diving into the deep end and trying to overcome your fears by sheer willpower isn't always the best approach.

Top myths and facts about spiders

Spiders have often been associated with fear and discomfort due to a variety of myths and misconceptions. However, it's important to separate fact from fiction and understand the truth behind these beliefs in order to overcome them.

Myth I: Spiders are dangerous

Fact: Despite their reputation, the reality is that the risk of being killed by a spider is incredibly low. In fact, it's estimated that only seven to ten people die worldwide each year due to spider bites. Most spiders are not dangerous to humans and only bite as a last resort, in self-defence.

Myth 2: Many spiders are venomous

Fact: This idea is widely held, but the truth is, only a tiny fraction of the estimated 40,000 to 50,000 species of spider in the world have venom that can cause harm to humans. And even among those, it's usually just the female spiders that pose a threat. So, you don't have to buy into the myth that all spiders are dangerous. The vast majority of these eight-legged creatures are not harmful, and there's no need to fear every spider you come across.

Myth 3: Spiders will attack

Fact: Spiders are not aggressive creatures and will only bite if they feel threatened. They are actually quite shy and prefer to avoid contact with humans whenever possible. Spiders do not have any malicious intent towards humans and are not out to get anyone, so don't worry about spiders coming after you.

Myth 4: Spiders can jump at you

Fact: Spiders do not have the ability to jump. They can only crawl or climb. It's important to understand their physical limitations and that they are not capable of jumping at a person from a distance. This fear is often fuelled by movies or television, but in reality spiders are not as agile or threatening as they are often portrayed.

Myth 5: Spiders are dirty and carry diseases

Fact: Spiders are actually very clean creatures and don't carry diseases that can be transmitted to humans. In fact, they eat disease-carrying insects like flies, making them good to have around.

Myth 6: Places with more spiders have more people with spider phobias

Fact: Research has shown that this is not the case. Individuals living in populated areas with dangerous spiders, versus those in areas without them, don't seem to experience any additional fear or anxiety on average.

Myth 7: You swallow eight spiders a year while you sleep

Fact: This is a common myth, but it's simply not true. Spiders aren't attracted to human food and don't crawl into people's mouths while they sleep, so don't worry about this one.

What is the danger from spiders?

Let's revisit the earlier number of approximately seven to ten people who die each year worldwide due to spider bites. It's a remarkably low figure. In fact, it represents only 0.0001 per cent of the total population. Now, compare that to getting attacked by a cow, which can cause serious injury or even death, with an estimated twenty-two deaths per year in the US. That's almost three times more likely than dying from a spider bite. And what about falling coconuts, which are responsible for an estimated 150 deaths per year worldwide. That's roughly fifteen times more likely than dying from a spider bite! If that's not enough, think about toasters. They can cause fires and burns, resulting in an estimated 4,000 fires per year in the US alone. That's approximately 400 times more likely than dying from a spider bite.

Causes of a fear of spiders

Despite the low risk of harm posed by spiders, it's not uncommon for people to experience a fear of these creatures. In Part I of this book, we explored how negative experiences or conditioning in the past can influence our feelings in the present. But what specifically can cause this type of conditioning to occur and what are some other factors that can contribute to a fear of spiders?

▶ Fear of the unknown ◀

Spiders can often look unnatural and move in ways that are unfamiliar and mysterious to us, leading us to fear them. This phenomenon is known as 'uncanny valley syndrome', where the less human-like an animal is, the more we tend to fear it. Our imagination can also play a big role in our fear of spiders, as we imagine hidden dangers and unknown aspects of spiders that we can't understand or explain. This fear of the unknown can be particularly intense, tapping into our primal instincts even if we know spiders aren't harmful. The unfamiliarity of spiders creates feelings of fear and uncertainty.

▶ Evolution ◀

The fear of spiders may have its roots in our evolutionary history, where species evolved to avoid dangerous things in the environment. This instinct has been passed down from generation to generation, and even though spiders pose no real threat today, our ancestors may have had good reason to fear them. Furthermore, research from various universities, including a 2022 study by Charles University and Amoud University, suggests that spiders may bear enough resemblance to their more dangerous relatives, scorpions, to trigger a similar fear response. This reaction is likely due to their comparable appearance and behaviour.

This instinctual fear is rooted in survival and self-preservation and highlights the importance of avoiding potential dangers in our environment.

▶ Negative media representations ◀

The media can significantly shape our perceptions of the world, especially when it comes to creatures like spiders. Sensationalized stories about the potential harm that spiders can cause can contribute to fear and anxiety among those who are unfamiliar with these creatures. False stories about harmful spiders appearing in areas and misdiagnoses of insect bites as spider bites that are spread on social media can further exacerbate these fears. This negative representation of spiders is also perpetuated in popular culture through the portrayal of spiders as dangerous and threatening in horror films and even in some films marketed towards younger audiences, such as arachnophobia and the earlier mentioned *Harry Potter* series. These depictions contribute to a negative image of spiders in the public eye.

► Culture ◄

Cultural beliefs and attitudes towards spiders can vary widely across different regions and cultures. In Western cultures, spiders are often associated with fear and revulsion, reinforced by the use of spider imagery in haunted house rides and Halloween parties to create a spooky atmosphere.

However, other cultures view spiders in a more positive light. For example, in some indigenous Australian cultures spiders are seen as powerful creatures with the ability to create and control webs, symbolizing the connections between people and the world. Spiders are also associated with creation stories and are seen as bringers of life and fertility. In these cultures, spiders are revered as spiritual beings and are considered protectors of the land and its inhabitants.

In some African and Native American cultures, spiders are viewed as symbols of creativity, resilience and patience. These cultural differences highlight how cultural beliefs can shape our experiences and emotions toward spiders.

► Other fears ◄

The fear of spiders can sometimes be connected to or intensified by other phobias. For instance, if you have a fear of germs, that could lead to a fear of spiders because they're often seen as unclean and contaminated. Despite the fact that spiders don't pose any germ-related risk, the belief that they do could trigger your fear of germs and make your spider phobia worse. After all, if you think you've come into contact with a spider, you may feel contaminated and want to cleanse yourself.

Another factor that may contribute to a fear of spiders is anticipatory anxiety or the fear of fear itself. If you're scared of being surprised or made to jump, you may experience that fear when thinking about spiders, even if your fear didn't start with them. And, if you have a fear of enclosed spaces or the dark, a fear of spiders could make those fears worse. This is because spiders are often associated with these types of environments and can trigger fear and anxiety in these situations.

Changing a fear of spiders

Early in my career I was called to a meeting with my bank manager. I was a little worried about what this might mean, but the manager greeted me with a warm smile, putting me at ease. The purpose of the meeting was to get to know the bank's customers better.

As I began to explain my work to the manager, she interrupted me with a question: 'Could you help me with my fear of spiders?' She had been struggling with this phobia for years, so I agreed to book a session with her.

Three months after the session, I returned for another meeting and asked her about her phobia. To my surprise, she reported that she hadn't seen any spiders and that this was unusual, as it was autumn and she had previously reported seeing one every day and going into a panic. After asking some more questions, I found out that she had visited a zoo with her family and gone into the insect house. 'Were there any spiders there?' I asked. 'Well, yes, there were,' she replied, 'but I didn't really notice them.' When I asked her how she would have felt three months prior, she said she wouldn't have gone near the place. This was the moment she realized her fear was gone and she hadn't even noticed.

I explained to her that her fear of spiders had put her on high alert, causing her to see potential threats everywhere. Once her brain realized that spiders were not actually dangerous, it stopped reacting with fear and she simply stopped noticing them.

This is an example of a deletion, which we covered in Part I, but this time for the positive.

People often ask me, 'How will I know when my phobia is gone?' The answer is simple: you'll often realize that you haven't noticed or thought about that thing in a while.

QUICK RECAP:

▶ Spiders pose a low risk to humans, with only a few reported deaths worldwide each year due to spider bites.

▶ Most of the 40,000 to 50,000 species of spider are harmless to humans, and other everyday items such as falling coconuts, toasters and even cows are much more likely to cause harm.

▶ Arachnophobia can be caused by several factors, including a fear of the unknown, evolutionary instincts, negative media representation, cultural beliefs or feelings of disgust.

FEAR OF ANIMALS

Zoophobia, as you might have guessed from the first part of the word, is a broad term used to describe a fear of animals and contains many more specific phobias within it.

If the thought of a snake slithering through the grass makes the hairs on the back of your neck stand up, a dog running up to you and putting its paws on you causes you to panic or even the thought of a mouse is enough to make you want to stand on a chair until it's gone, you might have zoophobia.

Fear of some animals makes sense from an evolutionary perspective. In the wild, we'd have no reason to want to be near an apex predator like a snarling tiger. We think rodents spread diseases and insects can have a nasty sting – but people with zoophobia can spin into a cycle of dread at just the mention of an animal.

While it's relatively rare for people to be scared of *all* animals, specific phobias related to one species or type of creature are incredibly common. These phobias can seriously impact people's wellbeing, but the fact that some people find animals totally benign can often mean they don't get taken seriously. A particularly memorable example of this was when I was running a workshop at a hotel next to a London park.

The closeness to the park meant the hotel's bar-cum-restaurant downstairs often played host to a parade of dog walkers. Early into the session, as I began laying the groundwork for the day's lesson, I noticed one person in the audience, Jess, reacting nervously, flinching and closing her eyes each time a dog barked – which was often.

On seeing this, I made the impromptu decision to shuffle the training agenda. After asking her privately if she was OK with my new idea, I decided to tackle her phobia there and then, using the fast phobia method you learned about in Step 5. As we began unpacking her fear, she recalled a childhood event that had sparked her fear of dogs (cynophobia).

During her primary school years, the police had visited to give a demonstration with their trained police dogs. Donned in protective padding, one officer allowed his dog to show how it took down a criminal. For her, this was a moment of terror that etched a deep mark on her psyche – the realization that dogs could attack.

What stood out for me was not the root of her fear, but how similar our childhood experiences were and how subjective and divergent our reactions can be – I too had seen an identical demonstration at my primary school. However, my interpretation had been polar opposite. I found a new admiration for the well-trained dog and its handler and even thought about pursuing a career as an animal handler as a result, whereas Jess had found abject terror. It's the perfect reminder that it's not the event, but *how we interpret* the event that determines how we feel.

She is far from alone – multiple celebrities have opened up and talked about how their fear of animals has affected them. Orlando Bloom discovered a fear of pigs, known as swinophobia, during the filming of *Kingdom of Heaven* when a pig somehow found its way onto the set and Bloom 'ran like crazy'. Phobias have also affected famous singers: Adele became afraid of seagulls after one violently stole an ice cream out of her hands, and Rihanna started to have panic attacks at the sight of fish, despite growing up on a Caribbean Island.

Myths about fear of animals
Myth I: Fear of animals means you hate them
<u>Fact</u>: This is entirely false – you can love animals and still be afraid of them. Phobias, by their very nature, do not occur in the rational thinking part of our minds but rather stem from our unconscious.

Myth 2: Fear of cats (ailurophobia) is only because of their association with bad luck in some cultures
<u>Fact</u>: While superstitions can contribute to fear, there can be many reasons for someone to develop ailurophobia, including past negative experiences or an aversion to certain behaviours or characteristics of cats.

Myth 3: Fear of dogs (cynophobia) only relates to big, intimidating ones
<u>Fact</u>: This fear can relate to every type of dog, regardless of their size, breed or behaviour. Someone with cynophobia could be sent into a panic by even the smallest puppy.

Myth 4: Fear of sharks (selachophobia) is mainly due to movies like Jaws
<u>Fact</u>: While such movies can undoubtedly contribute to fear, they are not the sole reason people develop fears like selachophobia. Personal experiences and the sharks' appearance and reputation as predators also play a part.

Myth 5: Fear of bats (chiroptophobia) is due to their association with vampires and the supernatural

Fact: This can contribute; however, fear of bats often has more to do with their nocturnal nature, the fact they're often found in dark, confined spaces and, more recently, that they might transmit diseases like COVID-19 – so much so that conservationists have been concerned with an increase in bat phobias causing people to hunt them down and kill them.

Myth 6: Fear of reptiles and amphibians (herpetophobia) is due to their skin texture

Fact: While the texture of these animals can contribute, herpetophobia is highly subjective. It could be related to the animal's appearance, the way they move, their behaviour or a misperception that they are venomous.

Myth 7: Fear of rodents (musophobia) comes from the fact they are inherently dirty and unhygienic creatures

Fact: Rodents like rats and mice are actually very diligent about their cleanliness and regularly groom themselves. The idea that they are dirty comes from their ability to survive in unhygienic urban environments, not from their natural behaviour. In a clean, cared-for setting, domestic rodents are typically clean and healthy.

The signs and causes of zoophobia

Like many phobias, zoophobia is often rooted in our childhood. Animals can also be hard to understand, and often we misinterpret their behaviours, like dogs jumping about or putting their paws on us when they want to play, as aggression. We might have experienced a traumatic event with an animal, such as a cat scratching us, or we might witness our parents reacting fearfully around animals, which can increase our likelihood of developing a phobia.

This was true for a journalist who came to see me, who had been deathly afraid of birds since childhood. Even in an open space she would get hot and her hands would tingle, and if she was in a more enclosed space she would often look to run away. While many people thought this was funny, it caused no end of embarrassment to her. It was so extreme that she would even feel uncomfortable around cooked chicken, causing her only to eat red meat, which, as we all know, isn't recommended for your health.

As we worked together on uncovering the root cause of her phobia, we discovered it wasn't a traumatic incident that triggered it. Instead, it was an encounter with her mother as they looked at a picture of cranes caught in a net. Her mother was terrified of birds, and the child found herself empathizing with her, relishing the rare closeness. Sharing a phobia unconsciously allowed her to develop an intimate connection with her mum. This is a type of secondary gain, which we covered in Step 3. Until we did the session, the journalist had no idea that her mother had played such a big role in the shaping of her phobia.

▶ Fear of animals from a historical perspective ◀

Fear of animals has a complex history that has been with us since the dawn of the human race. Many of us now have pet dogs, cats and hamsters, and cave paintings show that we were living alongside animals as early as the stone age. However, humans haven't always been apex predators, so our fear of animals was a very natural response to the very real threat they posed. Being afraid of a snake or other large predator wasn't just a phobia – it was a survival mechanism. I would imagine that most people, if you stood them next to a woolly mammoth, would be pretty scared – even more so if they had to hunt it for food! It's been suggested by evolutionary psychologists that this fear may have been passed down generationally, for it still to persist today.

Humans have always had some sort of relationship with animals, as they even took on a mythical reverence in some cultures, as they were seen as symbols and often connected with gods and goddesses. In ancient Egypt, cats were seen as representations of deities, and even accidentally killing one was considered a serious crime which could be punishable by death.

During the Middle Ages, our fear of animals crossed between superstition and religious belief. Black cats became associated with witchcraft and evil, leading to their mass persecution and killing. This superstition has been passed down, with many people still associating them with bad luck.

As some cultures began to travel further out into the world during the Age of Exploration, they suddenly started meeting new, exciting, scary animals. First encounters and subsequent stories with hippos, giraffes, lions and other unfamiliar creatures could have resulted in fearful tales being passed down through generations, and this also led to stories of mythical creatures such as the Kraken being perpetuated.

In more modern times, we have come to recognize that animals can be the carriers of disease, which could also reinforce our fears. If we truly believe a dog has rabies or a bat carries the next super-contagious viral infection, we're very likely to be scared. As advancements in psychology took place during the nineteenth and twentieth centuries, we began to recognize phobias as mental-health conditions rather than just irrational fear. Today, it's acknowledged that a combination of genetic factors, personal experiences and environmental influences can contribute to a person developing zoophobia.

▶ Culture ◀

Cultural attitudes towards domestic animals, such as cats and dogs, can shape perceptions and emotional responses. In societies where animals are primarily valued for utilitarian purposes, such as hunting or security, there tends to be more fear towards them. This is often the case in regions with higher populations of strays.

Conversely, in cultures where animals are seen as part of the family, they are often regarded with affection and familiarity. Growing up alongside a pet dog or cat can foster a sense of ease and comfort around these animals, reducing the likelihood of fear. For instance, a child who has never had a negative encounter with a pet is more likely to approach animals with openness and curiosity. What one culture deems a sensible wariness, another may view as an unfounded reaction.

▶ Interconnected fears ◀

Phobias often co-occur, and zoophobia is no different. It can blend with other fears and anxieties, creating a complex inner landscape. So, when we understand the fears that can connect with zoophobia we can start to navigate it more easily.

Often, zoophobia is tied to the fear of harm or death, with animals representing a threat to our safety. This is likely an evolutionary trait, and even though we don't encounter deadly animals on a daily basis, news stories about animal attacks, bites or diseases transmitted by animals can reinforce this fear. Fear of pain, injury or contracting a disease from an animal encounter also occurs frequently with zoophobia.

Zoophobia can also be linked to fearing the loss of our autonomy, with people scared that they might be incapacitated or disabled due to an animal attack. They might imagine a dog pinning them to the floor or a snake wrapping itself around them, rendering them helpless or overpowered.

Social phobia is also very tightly linked to zoophobia. No one likes losing their cool or thinking they look foolish in public, and people might be worried about appearing rude if someone has a pet. They might also fear dismissal, as some people might not understand why their loveable fluffy cat can strike immense fear into someone else.

Fear of animals can also be tied to their unpredictability, especially in the case of wild ones. This can spark fear in people who like being in control of their surroundings and can also relate to agoraphobia, or being scared of a situation that we might be unable to escape from.

Another journalist I worked with had a deep-seated fear of dogs. She had to avoid parks and walks in the country and would research stray dog populations when she was choosing a place to go on holiday. She had made a serious effort to get around her phobia using a number of therapies, but sadly with no success. Through working with me, she discovered that it wasn't just her belief that 'dogs are just plain scary' that was causing her fear, but also their unpredictability and her lack of ability to control them. It wasn't that she thought they were all inherently dangerous and out to get her, but they were unknown and unfamiliar.

We worked together using a number of the processes in this book, and after her first session she found herself surprisingly at ease in the presence of dogs. After another session, she could start to think about travelling to places with stray dogs and even started using dog-sharing apps. This goes to illustrate how once we peel back the layers and *really* start to understand the different components of our phobias, we can unravel them and reframe the way we experience the world.

QUICK RECAP:

▶ Zoophobia, the fear of animals, is a common condition affecting between 7 and 9 per cent of the population.

▶ The fear usually relates to a reaction to a specific animal species rather than to animals in general.

▶ The fear of animals can be evolutionary, cultural and individual in nature.

▶ The fear can extend beyond physical encounters to seeing pictures or even thinking about the feared animal.

▶ Misinterpretation of animal behaviours can amplify the fear, leading to avoidance and severe discomfort in the presence of animals.

▶ Zoophobia can co-occur with other fears and anxieties, such as fear of harm, death, loss of control, loss of autonomy and social phobia.

FEAR OF OPEN AND CLOSED SPACES

Fear of open spaces (agoraphobia) and fear of closed spaces (claustrophobia) are both fairly common phobias, affecting millions of people globally. It's estimated that 12 per cent of the world's population suffer from claustrophobia and 1.7 per cent from agoraphobia.

These two fears may seem at odds, but they share many things in common.

Both conditions can affect a person in several ways when sufferers think about or attempt to confront them. Similar experiences can trigger them and they are related to fears associated with space or lack thereof.

Claustrophobia is characterized by an irrational fear of being in enclosed or confined spaces. People with claustrophobia may fear being unable to breathe properly or being trapped, leading to panic attacks in situations where they feel confined, such as in an elevator or a small room.

Agoraphobia is often misunderstood as simply a fear of open spaces. More accurately, it involves a fear of being in situations where escape might be difficult or where help wouldn't be available if needed. This fear can manifest in open spaces like fields, but also in crowded areas, on public transportation or when far from a safe environment. The core issue is a concern for safety and the ability to escape or get help, not necessarily the type of space one is in.

Someone might experience both claustrophobia and agoraphobia together on the London Underground, for example, feeling the confinement of the train (claustrophobia) and simultaneously worry about the difficulty of getting to safety in the event of a panic attack (agoraphobia). Many people from history have suffered from these phobias, including the father of psychoanalysis Sigmund Freud and evolutionary biologist Charles Darwin. Additionally, celebrities such as Woody Allen, Justin Bieber and Paris Hilton, have all talked about having these phobias.

Hollywood star Uma Thurman has spoken about her challenges with claustrophobia in various publications. She explained that during the filming of *Kill Bill: Vol. 2* her character had to be buried alive and no acting was required for that particular scene. She said the screams were real; it was horrific and she was feeling genuine fear in that performance. While acknowledging her phobia, she is also quoted as saying, 'You don't need to be claustrophobic to fear being buried alive.'

Emma Stone also shared how she has suffered from agoraphobia since she was seven and has had many panic attacks. In an interview with Ellen DeGeneres, Emma talked about her intense panic when suddenly gripped by agoraphobia. She commented, 'Obviously, I knew there was no danger, but there was nothing in me that didn't think I was going to die.'

Myths and facts about claustrophobia and agoraphobia
Myth I: Claustrophobia is just a fear of small spaces
<u>Fact</u>: Claustrophobia isn't only a fear of small spaces. It can stem from a feeling of being trapped or suffocated and can be triggered by various situations.

Myth 2: Agoraphobics are introverted or antisocial people
<u>Fact</u>: Being agoraphobic doesn't necessarily mean you dislike people or crave solitude; more often it's about the fear of panicking in front of others.

Myth 3: If you have claustrophobia, you will fear all confined spaces
<u>Fact</u>: Many phobias can be very context-specific, and someone can be scared of one type of small space yet be perfectly OK with another. In the case of something like elevators, even the type of elevator may affect someone's reaction. For instance, is it old or new? Wide or narrow? Made of glass or metal?

Myth 4: If you genuinely had agoraphobia, you'd never be able to leave the house
<u>Fact</u>: If your agoraphobia is extreme, you may not be able to leave your house. However, some people can travel distances and to various outdoor places if they feel safe.

Myth 5: You are born with agoraphobia and claustrophobia
<u>Fact</u>: While most cases of claustrophobia or agoraphobia develop when you're young, sometimes they don't start until later.

Myth 6: Claustrophobia and agoraphobia are untreatable
<u>Fact</u>: As you have learned in this book, not only can these phobias be resolved but change can sometimes happen very quickly.

Myth 7: These phobias are always due to environmental triggers
Fact: This is not always the case as both internal and external factors can trigger claustrophobia and agoraphobia. A person might develop claustrophobia not because they were physically confined in a small space but due to internal feelings of vulnerability or lack of control during an event. Similarly, with agoraphobia it can stem from more than just environmental triggers; it may be related to past emotional entrapment, such as feeling powerless in a relationship.

The dangers and causes of claustrophobia and agoraphobia

When we look at space-related phobias, there is minimal risk, and they are more psychologically and emotionally based as opposed to physically threatening. That said, the impact of them can still be significant.

Claustrophobia can elicit fear whenever a person is confronted by the feeling or potential threat of being stuck. The danger lies in the potential for distress and the panic that can accompany it when faced with crowds, elevators, subways, caves or travel.

Going back to the fight or flight response discussed in Part I, in claustrophobia fear triggers the flight reaction as the person tries to run but realizes they are stuck. The adrenaline rush has nowhere to go and keeps the fear going.

With agoraphobia, the fear arises where escape may be difficult or help is far away. This can include public spaces, open areas or places where the person doesn't feel safe and fears the possibility of panicking. The dangers of these fears can extend beyond the immediate experience and can create a vicious cycle where fear leads to avoidance and avoidance feeds fear.

Another journalist client came to see me when she developed a fear of the London Underground. As she was based in the city, this caused her significant problems trying to get to work. Her fear started unexpectedly when her train was suddenly delayed. This single incident ignited a panic attack and changed a once routine journey into an unnerving daily experience.

The journalist was initially sceptical about whether I could help her, but she decided to come anyway. During our work together, she realized what she actually feared was her own reaction to the fear. She wrote about her work with me and said she was shocked that she was no longer panic-stricken on her commute and that her daily journey had again become uneventful. Her biggest takeaway was that she was no longer obsessively thinking about her journey on the Tube. This proves that people can quickly change their fears even if they are sceptical. It also goes to show that changing one belief can make a large impact on our phobias.

► Evolutionary roots ◄

The origins of claustrophobia and agoraphobia trace back to our evolutionary history. Humans have had to deal with various survival challenges, and like many other fears they could have served as a protection mechanism at some point in our past.

Early humans were cautious of tight, confined spaces as they could hide predators from view or slow them down. The need to avoid such small places may have been genetically passed on, contributing to the development of claustrophobia in certain people.

By comparison, fear of crowded places and the feeling of being unable to escape may have evolved if humans felt vulnerable to attacks from other people or predators. Open spaces would have meant less control over the environment in the wild, and additionally, having an overcrowded settlement could lead to famine or disease. This could have posed a significant problem to our ancestors, and the fear may have been encoded and passed down, even though these survival traits are significantly less necessary today.

▶ Media depictions ◀

Movies and shows can often overdramatize claustrophobia (like the *Kill Bill* example mentioned earlier). When music and other special effects are added, the depiction of being trapped, especially in horror movies, increases the drama and keeps the audience engaged and riveted to their seats. However, it can also increase the fear for someone who's struggling. When we look at agoraphobia, news and social media outlets can massively overestimate the risks around particular groups or places, increasing the fear in someone who is already nervous or anxious.

▶ Other phobias ◀

Existing anxieties and phobias can all exacerbate claustrophobia and agoraphobia in some people. Certain fears can overlap, and an individual who has a fear of heights could potentially develop claustrophobia or agoraphobia. For example, a person may avoid elevators because they're afraid of ascending to a great height, which can lead to the fear of elevators, creating claustrophobia. Similarly, they may avoid open spaces like balconies or rooftops due to a fear of heights, which can eventually evolve into a fear of open spaces if it's not dealt with effectively.

Someone with a germ phobia might fear large crowds and public places, and this was especially prominent during the COVID-19 pandemic. Individuals with a fear of public speaking may fear scrutiny and therefore have a tendency to avoid large crowds, leading them to develop agoraphobia.

Conversely, someone with a fear of being alone (monophobia) can also develop agoraphobia, as being in a space where no one can help and having no support can create fear. Additionally, if somebody has a predisposition towards anxiety, they're more likely to develop a fear of being trapped or of not being able to escape. They are also more likely to be highly attuned to their symptoms and therefore to the anticipation of discomfort or anxiety, which is likely to feed the problem.

▶ Cultural beliefs and attitudes ◀

Cultural beliefs can often shape people's response to confined or open spaces. High value is placed on personal space and privacy in some cultures, which might make some people far more susceptible to developing claustrophobia. Alternatively, in cultures where community living and close-knit ties are the norm, people might feel more comfortable in close quarters, reducing the likelihood of claustrophobia. However, they could potentially develop agoraphobia due to the anxiety associated with being away from their community and the support they get from that.

In some societies, attitudes towards travel and exploration are largely positive and encouraged, which could decrease the likelihood of developing these phobias; meanwhile, in cultures where exploration or venturing far from home is discouraged or seen as risky, it might increase the likelihood of developing either condition.

The frame

Agoraphobia and claustrophobia fall into the category of complex phobias, but that does not necessarily mean that the solution has to be complex.

I remember a client coming to see me who had developed a fear after being stuck in an elevator. As they described the incident, they talked as if they had been trapped for hours. However, as I guided them through the temporal reprocessing method, they realized they had actually been stuck for a relatively short time. This shift in perspective allowed them to gain a new understanding of their fear and change their perceptions.

The same thing often happens with a fear of the London Underground. My offices are in London's Harley Street, and this is one of the most common types of space-based phobias I deal with. Clients will often ask, 'What if the Tube gets stuck?' The first time I heard this, I asked them to think about how often that really happened. As we discussed it further, however, I realized they weren't talking about the Tube breaking down; they were referring to the train stopping for about thirty seconds during rush hour to iron out gaps in the service, which happens fairly often.

I did what I've done many times since. I explained that while to them this prompts a feeling of being trapped, for the driver and most passengers it's merely a thirty-second delay to ensure they don't crash into the train in front. Sometimes, simply doing the reframing technique can change the meaning we give our situation (as was the case with this client). By changing our perspective and the language we use to talk about our phobias, we can make significant changes to agoraphobia, claustrophobia – or any other phobia, for that matter.

QUICK RECAP:

▷ About 12 per cent of the world's population suffer from claustrophobia, and 1.7 per cent suffer from agoraphobia.

▷ Claustrophobia is associated with the fear of confinement, typically triggered by small or enclosed spaces. It can range from being physically trapped in a confined space to being emotionally trapped by feeling a lack of freedom or choice.

▷ Agoraphobia, which is often linked to panic attacks, involves fear of situations where escape might be difficult or embarrassing.

▷ These conditions can arise from various factors, including childhood experiences, traumatic incidents, genetic tendencies or evolutionary origins.

SOCIAL PHOBIAS

Social phobias encompass a range of fears that share the common element of a fear of negative judgement in social situations. These phobias can significantly restrict a person's engagement with the world and impair their ability to form meaningful connections with others.

For instance, erythrophobia, the fear of blushing, causes those affected to avoid eye contact or conversations, worried that any misstep could trigger a visible physical reaction.

Paruresis, or shy bladder syndrome, occurs when anxiety becomes overwhelming, making the natural act of using a public restroom a tense experience. Sufferers feel as though their most private moments are under public scrutiny.

Monophobia, the fear of being alone, stems from the concern that they are vulnerable without others' reassurance or the comfort of distraction. A humiliating moment, a history of bullying or prolonged stress can all contribute to the development of social phobias.

Of course, there is one social phobia that stands out for its ability to create fear: public speaking.

Fear of public speaking (glossophobia)

As I've already mentioned, I have had many phobias. Some naturally faded over time, but many needed to be worked on to let them go. Of all my phobias, speaking was one of the deepest rooted and one of the later ones I transformed.

Like many others, my fear of public speaking started in childhood. One day the teacher asked me to get up, come to the front of the class and read a section from a book. I was never all that great at reading, as I am dyslexic, so being forced to stand up in front of my classmates was scary. I stumbled through the lines and made a general mess of it. My nervousness fed my stumbling, and my stumbling caused me to make more mistakes, which created a vicious cycle of fear.

Of course, children being children, a group at the back began laughing at me, and I just wanted the ground to open up and swallow me. Aside from feeling totally humiliated and embarrassed, this specific incident triggered the belief that public speaking was something to avoid at all costs.

As I went through the rest of my childhood and progressed into college, this fear became a real issue. I used to avoid making presentations, even if they sometimes cost me a passing grade. On one occasion, I tried calming my nerves with too much Dutch courage. As you can imagine, this didn't go down well, ultimately making things a lot worse. I stumbled over my words, and the alcohol made the incident stick in my mind even more.

Later in life, I reached the tipping point that allowed me to let go of my fear, In fact, fast forward about thirty years, and there I was on BBC One. They had invited me onto a prime-time TV show to work with the presenter's mother, who feared reading on stage, and her fear had been triggered the same way as mine. As a child, she had been forced to stand up and read at school, and it hadn't gone well.

Despite having this phobia for a very long time, in the space of just over an hour she went from being scared of even walking into the school or holding a book to being able to calmly and confidently read on stage in front of an audience. She gained a sense of freedom she'd never had before.

See the video here.

Our voice is one of the most powerful tools at our disposal, yet, ironically, using it can often be one of the most daunting tasks imaginable. For many, public speaking is a challenge that ranks alongside the most frightening things to do. It's an arena that simultaneously demands vulnerability and conviction and where we face our fears of judgement, rejection and self-perceived incompetence.

Staggeringly, an estimated 75 per cent of people grapple with a fear of public speaking. Also known as glossophobia, this condition can be so severe that, in a 1973 study by Bruskin Associates, public speaking was ranked as a more significant fear than death by participants. Subsequent research has corroborated these findings to some extent; however, when directly asked to choose between the fear of death and public speaking, more individuals identified death as the greater fear. Nonetheless, the fact that public speaking consistently emerges as a fear at the top of people's minds illustrates its distressing nature for so many. Many people find these facts surprising, especially that people's fear is so high, given that speaking to a group typically poses no physical risk of harm.

If you've ever felt your heart pound at the thought of standing before an audience, take comfort in knowing you're in good company. Elton John, Rod Stewart, Barbara Streisand, Andrea Bocelli and Donny Osmond all did or still now fear public appearances and speaking in front of people. Harrison Ford, the star of Hollywood blockbusters like *Star Wars* and *Indiana Jones*, has referred to public speaking as 'a mixed bag of terror and anxiety'.

Myths and facts about public speaking
Myth 1: Public speaking can only take place on a stage
Fact: If you break it down, 'public speaking' is just the act of speaking in front of others. We all do this at one time or another, and many of us do it daily. It doesn't have to involve microphones or stages, either. Speaking in public includes chatting in a bar with your friends, giving a speech at a wedding, asking questions in front of other people and – increasingly – talking on platforms like Zoom, Microsoft Teams, Skype etc. When you think about it, even speaking to the cashier in front of other shoppers at your local supermarket is public speaking.

Myth 2: You need lots (and lots!) of practice
Fact: Getting practice can boost your self-confidence, and joining your local Toastmasters group can significantly build that confidence, but you don't need lots of practice before speaking in public. In fact, getting obsessed with practising (and being perfect) can mean that you never put yourself out there at all because you can always find reasons for not being good enough.

Myth 3: You have to memorize a script
Fact: Some of the best speeches can be impromptu, and people respond well when you get up and speak on impulse. Speaking

from the heart with feeling and authenticity will always get a better response than something scripted.

Myth 4: Public speaking is going to be a humiliating or embarrassing experience

Fact: Public speaking can leave you feeling exhilarated, yet people only usually tell us about their negative experiences because those make the most entertaining stories.

Myth 5: The best public speakers never feel nervous

Fact: There's a misconception that seasoned public speakers never feel nervous or anxious before a speech. The truth is, even the most experienced speakers still experience nerves before they go on stage. The difference is they've learned how to manage these nerves and use them as a source of energy and enthusiasm. So, if you feel nervous before a speech, remember that it's a normal part of the process and can even enhance your performance if channelled properly.

Myth 6: The audience is going to test you

Fact: Many people approach public speaking with the mindset that the audience is out to judge them harshly or criticize their every move, which can create unnecessary anxiety and pressure. The truth is most audience members are there because they are interested in what you have to say, and they want you to succeed. Instead of viewing the audience as your adversary, try to see them as your ally. They're not there to see you fail but to learn from you.

What are the dangers and causes of fear of public speaking

In many phobias, there is often an underlying risk that has been blown out of proportion. Realistically, the worst that can happen when you're speaking is freezing up, forgetting what you want to say, or being embarrassed by something. Even if that were to happen, though, you'd still walk away in one piece; no actual harm can come to you. With this phobia, it's really all about ego: the fear of being judged, of not fitting in, of being rejected by the group, of being in the spotlight and so on. Of course, that doesn't make it any less real. I know only too well how much power this fear can have over your life and choices.

▶ Triggers ◀

As with myself and many of my clients, fear of public speaking can start from a negative trigger while speaking or performing as a child, but other factors can create this phobia too.

Sometimes it's less to do with you speaking and more about the audience's reaction. I have worked with many people who had a fear of public speaking but who weren't afraid of actually getting up and talking. Their real fear was around how the audience might react, and especially being judged. For example, 'Will they laugh? Will they get angry? Will they get bored or heckle me?', and this is often tied to a social phobia.

Being unable to cope with your own reactions sometimes plays a role in this fear too. What you're really worried about isn't how the audience will react but how you will if something goes wrong. Maybe the fearful person went through a time when they were under tremendous pressure and they got overwhelmed when they suddenly had to do a presentation for their boss or colleagues, making them panic. So, whenever they think about speaking to a group now, even if they're not under pressure, they worry that they'll panic and freeze again.

Another trigger is being trapped, and the moment the door shuts behind you and the lights in the auditorium are dimmed, the terror sets in:

▶ What will happen if something goes wrong?

▶ Can you get to the door?

▶ Will you have to walk past your audience – maybe even your boss – while they're laughing at you?

▶ What if the door gets stuck, and you make a fool of yourself trying to open it?

And so it goes on. Another trigger can be perfectionism. It's normal to feel anxious when worrying about making mistakes or forgetting key points, yet for many there is a tendency to strive for perfection, which can make things unbearably difficult, even though audiences tend to overlook minor mistakes or may even perceive them as a way to connect with the speaker on a more human level. Additionally, imposter syndrome is something else that frequently adds to the fear of public speaking. We will cover more about imposter syndrome later as it relates to our discussion on the fear of success and failure.

▶ History ◀

Our ancestors needed to blend into a small, tight-knit group for survival purposes. They made sure not to do anything embarrassing to avoid standing out negatively, and the fear of public speaking may be rooted in this, as the possibility of being ostracized for not fitting in with the tribe could mean being left behind and ultimately death. Therefore, anything that made you stand out from the crowd or made you the centre of attention was to be avoided, so fear of public speaking could be seen as a survival mechanism handed down through generations despite its original context no longer applying today.

▶ Cultural beliefs and attitudes ◀

Authority and leadership can be demonstrated through public speaking in certain cultural or societal expectations. However, if you feel you don't meet the societal standards or cultural expectations attached to public speaking, this could create fear. People with strong accents, women and individuals from minority groups express anxiety about speaking in public due to fears of discrimination or bias.

QUICK RECAP:

▸ Glossophobia, or the fear of public speaking, affects roughly 75 per cent of people. This fear often originates from childhood incidents or negative speaking experiences, and it's closely tied to the fear of judgement or embarrassment.

▸ Despite popular misconceptions, public speaking is not exclusive to naturally confident individuals or professionals, doesn't necessitate a script and can occur in everyday situations.

▸ High-profile personalities like Elton John and Barbra Streisand have also faced this fear.

FEAR OF TRAVELLING

For most people who love adventure and exploration, travel offers fresh opportunities, diverse cultural experiences, beautiful landscapes and the creation of lifelong memories. However, for others the idea of travelling is accompanied by feelings of dread. Known as travel phobia, or hodophobia, this refers to a spectrum of travel-related fears that can include aviation-based (aerophobia), vehicle-based (vehophobia) and watercraft-based (naviphobia) modes of transport. Additionally, if somebody fears being away from home, they might encounter generalized anxieties or panic attacks (agoraphobia).

The reasons behind a travel phobia can vary. Things like encountering new environments, meeting different cultures and linguistic obstacles can be overwhelming for some people. The fear of leaving the safety and familiarity of home can also contribute to travel-related fears, and apprehension around safety or motion-related illness can worsen existing travel phobias, substantially in some cases.

This phobia can affect growth and freedom. Aside from being

unpleasant, it holds you back from pursuing careers where travelling may be required and creating great memories through exploring the wonders the world has to offer.

Fear of flying (aerophobia)

Long before I became a therapist I worked as a cameraman, and one of my assignments was a documentary about snowboarders. This was in the days before camera drones, so getting aerial footage of a group of snowboarders coming down a mountain meant getting in a helicopter to film them. It was the last day of the shoot, so that night everyone celebrated, and the next day we travelled home, returning a few weeks later to get additional shots to complete the documentary. While we were at our hotel, someone mentioned the helicopter I had flown in on on my last visit had crashed just thirty minutes after dropping me off.

Initially, it didn't bother me; after all, accidents happen all the time, so what difference did it make whether it was thirty minutes or a week later? However, this blasé outlook didn't last very long. While I was out with the snowboarders the next day, one of them became very serious and pointed over towards a black streak on the side of a nearby mountain. 'You see those scorch marks?' he said. 'That's where the helicopter you were in last time crashed. Man, you were so lucky you got off it when you did.'

The image burned deep into my subconscious as I stared at the blackened snow and the charred tree stumps, thinking, 'That could have been me.'

After that, I couldn't even go near an airplane, and this became another phobia that affected me for many years. Luckily, I'm free from this fear now and recently I even took flying lessons.

Today, I have helped many people with their fear of flying. In fact, it's become one of my specialties. It might not seem like an important phobia to work on, as flying can be easily avoided with little impact on day-to-day life; however, it's one of those fears where you don't realize how much you're missing until you let it go.

A client contacted me once, desperate to resolve their fear of flying. They felt their marriage hadn't started yet as they couldn't take their honeymoon because they couldn't get on a plane. It had been over a year and it was putting a strain on their relationship; it felt like their relationship was on the rocks. We worked together to remove the phobia, and after they'd been on honeymoon they took a number of other trips abroad. They said it was, in a word, transformative.

The fear of flying is not that uncommon. It is estimated that about 20–25 per cent of individuals dislike being on planes, and roughly one in ten suffer from severe fear when it comes to flying. Many famous people, including Jennifer Lawrence, Jennifer Aniston, Ben Affleck, Sandra Bullock and Colin Farrell, struggle with this too.

Sean Bean is a British actor best known for his roles in fantasy films and TV shows like *The Lord of the Rings* and *Game of Thrones*. Despite playing tough warrior roles, he doesn't cope well with flying.

It was reported that when filming *The Fellowship of the Ring* in New Zealand, the actors had to take a helicopter to various locations, and his fear of flying was so bad that he chose to hike or travel by donkey rather than get in the helicopter.

And in the world of sport, Dutch footballer Dennis Bergkamp feared flying so badly it earned him the nickname 'The Non-Flying Dutchman'. He reportedly declined to participate in away games that required air travel, including some important Champions League fixtures and World Cup matches.

Myths and facts about flying

Myth I: Flying is dangerous

Fact: In reality, flying is the safest way to travel compared to other forms of transport. The chances of being killed in an air crash are around 1/5,000,000 to 1/20,000,000, and the stats get better yearly. To put that in context, according to the *Guardian* you are 100 times more likely to die travelling on the road than in a plane. In fact, more people are killed by lightning strikes each year than by plane crashes, and some years there are no deaths in commercial aviation incidents at all.

Myth 2: But it happens to somebody

Fact: Each year, around 60 million people die around the world, which is about eight people out of every 1,000, but only a tiny fraction of those die in airplane accidents, and in truth the fear of flying is far more likely to kill you than flying itself. I'm not just talking about the health effects of fear and stress: after the attacks on the World Trade Center, large numbers of Americans switched from flying to driving, and as a result in the twelve months after 9/11 the number of people killed in road traffic accidents increased by almost 1,600. If you're still thinking, 'It has to happen to somebody!', dying from mosquito bites (1 in 55), alcohol and drugs (1 in 34), or heart disease (1 in 4 people) are far higher and much more likely for most of us.

Myth 3: If an airplane crashes, it's over – you can't walk away. At least in a car accident, there's a chance you'll get out alive

Fact: Fatal plane crashes in which everyone dies make big news headlines, but they are incredibly rare. According to the US National Transportation Safety Board, you have a 95.7 per cent chance of walking away from a plane crash.

Myth 4: Airlines aren't affected by crashes, so they don't care

Fact: It's a mistake to assume that airlines don't feel any pain in the event of a crash. Financially, even the cheapest commercial airliners cost upwards of $80 million, and compensation costs in the wake of an airplane accident can also run to millions. Beyond that, behind the brand are human beings who feel guilt and remorse when something happens to the people who travel with them, and pilots and crew also want to come home to their families.

Myth 5: If an engine fails, the plane will fall from the sky

Fact: Think about gliders here. They're planes without engines, and yet they fly. It's not the engines that keep a plane up; it's the air movement over the wings. So, even if all the engines were to fail simultaneously (which is almost unheard of), it would become a big glider. Indeed, a plane flying at a typical cruising altitude (36,000 feet) could glide 60 miles without engines.

Commercial pilots practise gliding all the time, and every time an airliner lands there's a part of the descent where the pilots reduce the engine power to a minimum and allow the plane's momentum to take them in. Even if your worst nightmare does happen and the engine cuts out, your pilot has had rigorous training to teach them how to land safely.

Myth 6: Turbulence is dangerous

Fact: Have you ever watched water in a stream? The water continuously moves, and although it flows in one direction (downstream), it doesn't all move at the same rate or follow the same path. If you look carefully you see little whorls and eddies in the water, and if you come to a point where two streams meet, the water gets even more turbulent.

The air around a plane is exactly the same. It's full of currents and air streams, some moving at different speeds and some in different directions. And just like the whorls and eddies in a stream, they create turbulence when two masses of air moving differently meet. Turbulence to a pilot is like waves to the captain of a boat. It's just part of flying. When your plane enters a turbulent patch, it can seem scary, but the worst that's likely to happen is you'll end up with your drink in your lap.

Myth 7: Lightning can bring down a plane

Fact: While lightning occasionally hits planes, they are designed to withstand it, and no modern commercial aircraft have been brought down by lightning. So, if it does strike, sit back and enjoy the view; it can be pretty spectacular seeing things from that height.

Myth 8: The wing of the plane might fall off

Fact: The plane's design allows the wings to bend, and they are stress tested before an aircraft is even allowed to fly. In one test, the wings of a Boeing 787 were flexed 25 feet upwards – the equivalent of 150 per cent of the most extreme forces a plane would ever be expected to encounter in normal operation – and the wings stayed firmly attached!

Myth 9: If flying is so safe, why do I keep seeing plane crashes on the news?

Fact: I was browsing the internet a few years ago and someone had shared a video of a plane crash where, sadly, six people were killed. Even though it was a small private plane, thousands of people shared the video, it got millions of views, and worried clients contacted me about it.

Some time later, I was going out and saw the police had cordoned off the end of the road. The cordon tape was gone when I got home, and everything was back to normal. I searched the web to find out what had happened but couldn't find anything. Eventually, a few days later, a neighbour told me there had been a serious car crash and six people had died.

Now, here's the thing. I probably wouldn't have known about the car crash if I hadn't been walking down the street that day. The same number of people died, but no one shared videos on social media. There weren't scary images and headlines in the media. It barely registered – but why? Quite simply, it's not big news because people die in car crashes all the time. In fact, in most cases, car crashes don't even make the local newspaper.

Flying is so safe that when there is an incident, it's major news, and aviation accidents tend to stay in the headlines for several days afterwards, making them seem even worse.

In reality, there are over 100,000 flights per day (you can see how many aircraft are in the air at any time at FlightRadar.com), and you can see them taking off and landing without incident.

What is a phobia of flying?

While two people may fear flying, they likely have very different phobias when you look deeper. A fear of flying could be a fear of:

- Heights

- Turbulence/movement

- Being confined and not being able to get off the plane

- Falling or crashing

- Being scared of embarrassing yourself

- Loss of control

And these aren't mutually exclusive: your fear of flying might comprise several things, not just one. Let's look at these in more detail.

If you have increased anxiety levels during take-off or when reaching a certain altitude, it may suggest that acrophobia (fear of heights) is present.

The unpredictability of motion often leads to people fearing turbulence (kinetophobia), so if you are worried about abrupt changes in altitude or are terrified of air pockets during the flight, this could explain it. With that said, fear of situations with sudden and uncontrollable movements might not only be flying; you may also fear activities such as roller coaster rides or travelling at speed.

Claustrophobia is likely at play if you experience heightened anxiety when considering being confined on an airplane without any available exits. If your fear starts when the doors begin to close or you start worrying about the plane's size, this may be the problem. It's also likely you get these feelings in small spaces like elevators or tunnels.

If you are scared about the plane crashing, you might suffer from fear of falling (basophobia), or if you have asthenophobia – fear of showing any kind of physical weakness – you may have catastrophic thoughts that involve imagining the worst possible outcome when flying.

If you experience anxiety because you're not piloting the plane or cannot see what's happening, you may be uncomfortable with the unknown, and you'd likely get intense anxiety when visualizing uncontrollable circumstances, otherwise known as anticipatory anxiety – which probably isn't just when flying but in many areas of your life.

The BBC reached out to me to be part of their show called *Skies Above Britain* and asked me to help a woman who had an extreme fear of flying, and they flew her down from Scotland to work with me. With a large camera in my face, the director said, 'OK, let's see what you can do; we'll be flying her back soon.' The pressure was on. At this point, I didn't know just how bad she had felt flying down to London the day before. She said she'd been terribly stressed and tearful and very scared. We worked on her fear, and then she left for the airport and got on a plane to travel home.

It wasn't until a year later, when the show was broadcast on TV, that I got to see the parts I wasn't privy to at the time (her flight down and back). I saw her transformation from being terrified before our session to the return flight, where she was confident, fearless and happy.

If you didn't know what we had done, you could be forgiven for thinking it was due to magic or voodoo, when in fact I just helped her reshape her subconscious responses towards flying. I helped her change how her brain connected terror with flying and instead linked it to calmness and relaxation. I also helped her realize she was able to handle any unpredictable events. Her fear of flying was about being out of control, but for other people the one fear can be made up of many different types of phobias.

▶ Media depictions ◀

The news has hyped the risk of flying for many people. The Lockerbie crash in the UK, 9/II in the USA and Ethiopian Airlines Flight 302 were on our screens for months and became embedded into people's minds. Additionally, documentaries like *Air Crash Investigation* have not helped with this fear.

While unsettling, these real-life incidents do not accurately depict how rare accidents are or how safe air travel is.

On top of this, movies can have a dramatic impact on distorting the possible dangers too. Hollywood loves to portray catastrophic plane crashes in the most dramatic way possible. Movies like

Flight, Airplane! and *Final Destination* trigger many people's fear of flying. And survival movies like *The Grey* and TV shows like *Lost* work as a great filmic shorthand to put the protagonists in unfamiliar territory with unknown people. However, it's important to remind ourselves these programmes are fictional. It would be like trying to gauge the likelihood of developing a serious illness, getting divorced or having a major drama occur in your life by using soap operas as a guide.

It's common for people to watch movies and view scenes where cars crash through several buildings and come out unscathed. We know special effects were used, and we dismiss the act as impossible; however, when some people watch depictions of airplane crashes on film and television shows, they question whether what they see could actually happen.

Movies and news headlines typically sensationalize to captivate their audience, but the portrayal of air travel on screen typically doesn't match real-life reality.

▶ History ◀

In the early twentieth century, air travel was still a relatively new and unfamiliar mode of transportation, so there was a general apprehension and fear surrounding flying, and during the early years of aviation safety standards and technology were not as advanced as they are today. Accidents and crashes were more frequent, leading to a heightened perception of risk associated with flying.

As aviation technology advanced and safety measures improved, the overall safety of flying increased significantly. However, fears surrounding flying persisted due to memorable and highly publicized aviation disasters that occurred throughout history. Fear of flying can also be influenced by broader historical events and cultural shifts as well. For instance, during times of heightened security measures, such as in the aftermath of terrorist attacks, concern usually increases about safety and the potential for further incidents.

That said, it is important to remind yourself that the overall safety record of air travel has steadily improved over time, and it gets safer year after year.

QUICK RECAP:

▶ Fear of flying – experienced by approximately 20–25 per cent of individuals – typically consists of a combination of phobias, such as acrophobia (fear of heights), kinetophobia (fear of motion), claustrophobia (fear of enclosed spaces) and agoraphobia (fear of lack of control).

▶ Sensationalized media portrayals and misunderstandings about flying often amplify this fear, despite air travel being one of the safest modes of transportation.

▶ The odds of being involved in a fatal air travel accident are extremely low.

▶ It's important to remind yourself of the contrast between historical aviation risks, media representation, past triggers and the actual safety of modern air travel.

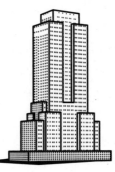

FEAR OF HEIGHTS

Acrophobia – a profound, irrational fear of heights – has existed as long as humans have.

In theory, fear of heights makes sense. After all, falling from a great height can injure or even kill us. However, most of us aren't regularly exposed to heights in a dangerous context – strict health and safety laws protect us. It's unlikely that the elevator you're in will plummet to the ground, and the skyscraper you're at the top of is unlikely to crumble. Still, I deal with people paralyzed with fear even at the mere mention of heights.

Imagine that you're standing at the edge of a tall building. Some of us might experience a feeling of apprehension or dread, and others may feel a thrill at being so close to danger. But this situation is a nightmare if you're living with acrophobia.

Most of us will naturally have some trepidation around heights (you wouldn't catch me climbing a building without proper safety gear!). With acrophobia, though, even the thought of being in a high place provokes intense anxiety, physical sensations such as a racing heart and dizziness, and frustration and helplessness, especially when the person feels they are in mortal danger but knows the fear is irrational.

One of the most unlikely people I thought would ever walk through my door was a professional stuntman called Max. He was well known for his fearless appearances on-screen but carried a secret; he had harboured a deeply entrenched fear of heights for his entire career.

This phobia, as ironic as it seemed considering his profession, had serious implications for his career. His fear was specific to freestanding heights like cliff edges or building tops, an aspect of acrophobia known as 'visual height intolerance'. His phobia meant he had to reject certain roles, limiting his opportunities in the industry.

Max had never experienced a fall or accident from a significant height, and it had nothing to do with the possibility of harm – he was pretty happy to drive a motorbike at 100mph while on fire.

We traced the origin of the fear back to his childhood. His construction worker father often narrated his work experiences, embellishing the dangers of working at great heights. Over time, these narratives unconsciously shaped Max's fear, creating a phobia that was completely opposed to his fearless image.

After we worked together, he could perform breathtaking high-altitude stunts without any fear (although I've changed his name here, there's a good chance you've seen him in a film recently!).

This fear can affect people from all walks of life – singer Jessie J famously had to overcome her fears to perform on a raised stage, and *Spider-Man* actor Tobey Maguire ironically struggled with heights while filming his stunts for the movie series. He said that despite his character's love of swinging between rooftops, 'standing on the edge of a building, looking over the edge – it's so horrible. I hate it.'

Matt Damon, known for his roles in action-heavy flicks such as the *Bourne* series, found he had a dormant fear of heights when filming at the top of a tall building in Dubai, recounting, 'We get up to the top and we go out on the pad and start walking towards the edge, and my legs were completely frozen. I couldn't physically move; it was crazy.' And this was despite all the safety procedures in place. This particular example illustrates the conflicting feelings that phobias bring up in us – our conscious mind knows we are perfectly safe, but our unconscious is still ringing alarm bells.

If you suffer from acrophobia, it can dictate where you choose to live and how you spend your leisure time, or hold you back from taking jobs you've worked hard for, which was the reality for Sarah.

Sarah was a seasoned businesswoman who had always been gripped by a paralyzing fear of heights. She was a high achiever in most aspects of her life – she had a degree from a prestigious university, a great career and was, for all intents and purposes, very successful. Still, something was standing in her way – a fear of heights. She was constantly headhunted and received multiple job offers, but there was always one problem: they were always in high-rise buildings.

Realizing this was holding her back immensely, Sarah decided to come and see me. After working together, situations she once dreaded were faced with calmness and even pleasure. The crippling anxiety and worry that once dictated her actions were no more. She could fulfil her dreams and take on the positions she had worked so hard to get. Our phobias affect us in myriad ways, and letting go of them unlocks so much more than peace of mind. By dealing with the phobia, Sarah also achieved her career goals, hit her earning targets and felt more satisfied with life overall. It was never about trying harder; it was just about moving on.

Myths and facts about acrophobia
Myth I: Acrophobia is rare
<u>Fact</u>: Acrophobia is actually one of the most common phobias.

According to Huppert et al., around 33 per cent of the general population experience some form of height intolerance or acrophobia. A poll by YouGov found that 58 per cent of adults report some degree of fear of heights.

Myth 2: If you have acrophobia, you can't go upstairs or climb a ladder

Fact: A study in the *Journal of Anxiety Disorders* showed that people with acrophobia could do relatively risk-free tasks like climbing stairs or ladders without major issues. However, some people may struggle with extreme heights or situations where falling would have severe consequences.

Myth 3: Acrophobia is just a fear of falling

Fact: While it's clear that fear of falling is a large part of acrophobia, it's not that open-and-shut. In fact, the fear of falling has its own name (basophobia), and this fear revolves around the sensation of falling rather than the height.

Sometimes, acrophobia is accompanied by the fear of losing control or the fear of the vastness of open spaces, and the risk to physical health is often overshadowed by the psychological impact of feeling overwhelmed and helpless.

Myth 4: You're born with acrophobia

Fact: While some people may show signs of a fear of heights from birth, it can develop at any stage in our lives. I often work with people who have experienced some form of trauma related to height, and this doesn't just mean a fall. It could be having a panic attack, feeling trapped or even someone playing an ill-advised prank. It's also worth noting that having pre-existing phobias can lead to an increased risk of acrophobia.

Myth 5: People with acrophobia are more likely to be fearful in other areas of their lives

Fact: To the contrary, acrophobia is a specific phobia, a mental and physical reaction to certain stimuli. Just because you're scared of heights doesn't mean you are scared in general – many people I treat have plenty of adventurous hobbies.

Myth 6: If you have acrophobia, you can't have anything to do with heights

Fact: In reality, acrophobia doesn't have to hold you back from achieving your goals. One of my favourite examples is Gustave Eiffel, the designer of the Eiffel Tower, who was famously scared of heights. However, this didn't stop him from creating one of the tallest (at the time) and most iconic constructions ever achieved.

Myth 7: Vertigo and acrophobia are one and the same

Fact: It's easy to get these two mixed up, but they're different entities. Vertigo is a physical sensation, often spurred by inner-ear or brain complications, that triggers feelings of imbalance and spinning. While heights can trigger it, that doesn't make it synonymous with a fear of heights.

Myth 8: Any fear of heights is an instant acrophobia diagnosis

Fact: Here's the thing – a pinch of fear when peering over the edge of a skyscraper is our natural survival instinct at work. Acrophobia is an entirely different ball game. It's an intense, irrational fear that inserts itself into daily life without any reason or logic. That said, it shares similarities with other fears, so it's always worth delving deeper into the root cause.

One client I had recently who was not a typical client (although there is no such thing as a *typical* phobia client) was Joe. Joe didn't have a background of experiencing particular phobias or even fear around heights, but he came to me convinced that he did.

He thought this fear must have laid dormant until he went on holiday and was encouraged to experience a 'terror bridge' – a bridge over a vast gap with only clear plexiglass on the floor, providing a perfect view of what you'd be falling onto should the structure fail. Now, being scared of a terror bridge seems normal, but with Joe it left a lasting impression.

He saw elderly families and young children all cross the bridge without any problems, but when it came to his turn he was left shaking on the side, unable even to put his feet on it. Convinced that this was a huge fear of heights, he came to see me. We discovered that the underlying cause was a fear of being judged – Joe couldn't allow himself to be nervous in public. He thought that everyone would be laughing at him, so he bottled the emotions up until they overwhelmed him. His perceived acrophobia was actually social anxiety.

What are the dangers and causes of a fear of heights?

Like all phobias, a fear of heights is often rooted in culture and biology. Let's look at this in more detail.

▶ Heights from a historical perspective ◀

You don't need to be an expert on psychology to deduce that being wary of heights might have started as a safety mechanism against falling from high places. Imagine being an early human foraging for food up a tree – one slip could be fatal. Some healthy fear triggered by this situation would ensure that you would take as much care as possible; however, this instinctual fear response, honed over millennia, has carried into the modern day, manifesting in some of us as acrophobia.

Vivid descriptions of the fear of heights can be found in ancient texts from the Greek, Roman and Chinese classics; acrophobia is derived from the Greek words *akron*, meaning peak or summit, and *phobia*, signifying fear.

Even now, tales give currency to heights as something to be scared of. We've all heard the dangers of flying too close to the sun, which refers to the Greek myth of Icarus plunging from the sky as the man-made wax wings he used to escape prison melted.

Our fear responses are not purely instinctual, though. Our everyday experiences can significantly influence our reaction to heights or open spaces. For instance, in societies where tall structures like urban cityscapes are a common part of everyday life, the fear of heights might be less prevalent than in cultures where people live closer to the ground.

▶ Triggers ◀

If we want to understand the nature of acrophobia, we need to recognize what triggers it, what could potentially cause it and the signs that indicate its presence.

Sometimes we are at increased risk of developing acrophobia, if it's linked to a traumatic event in our past, such as falling or watching someone else fall from a height, having a negative experience like a panic attack, or a medical emergency. New research has suggested that the root cause of fear of heights could lie within our genes. DNA testing company 23andMe found that there are a total of 392 genetic markers associated with fear of heights.

It's been found that people with a fear of heights will see a surface as nearly twice its real height as opposed to someone without the fear – this is known as evolved navigation theory.

QUICK RECAP:

▶ Many people struggle with acrophobia, and it is far beyond just the fear of falling. This discomfort is not limited to physical heights but extends to even the thought of being in high places, resulting in palpable fear.

▶ Fear of heights can have a multitude of different causes, ranging from past trauma to genetic predisposition.

▶ It's highly unlikely that heights will cause us harm unless we work in certain niche industries.

MEDICAL PHOBIAS

In my career, I'm lucky enough to have met a huge range of people and have held sessions with those who struggled with medical phobias that present in very different ways. Medicine is a huge field covering everything from dentistry to surgery to maternal care, and as such the landscape of related phobias (together known as iatrophobia) and their causes is just as diverse and complex.

Some people would faint at the sight of needles or blood, others obsess and ruminate over germs or the possibility of getting a very specific illness; other people watch everything they eat because of a fear of choking and other people because of a fear of vomiting. I've worked with a client who would be sent into a cycle of dread at the sound of a rubber glove being snapped on. I've had clients whose hearts would start racing at the thought of a doctor's appointment, others who might be triggered by the smell of hospital disinfectant, and some who absolutely couldn't stand the thought of a dentist touching their teeth.

A lady I worked with on live TV fell into this latter category;

the TV company had reached out to me about helping her with a crippling fear of dentists. She was so scared that she had made a promise she would never step foot in one again, and even thinking about one was enough to make her cry. But she had severe tooth problems that were leaving her in agony and could lead to serious health conditions.

We did our intervention live on air, and as we got into her past we found the traumatic events that had caused her problems in the first place. After doing some work around this, her confidence had risen to the point she actually managed to attend her important dental appointments and address her long-neglected issues. She was able to see that the dentist wasn't there to cause her pain but to offer a solution to it.

She's not alone in having medical phobias; martial arts actor Jackie Chan once snapped his own finger back into place rather than face the possibility of seeing a needle. *The Hobbit* actor Martin Freeman has a fear of choking – he can't eat avocados for fear of the stone getting caught in his throat – and Cameron Diaz has a well-publicized fear of vomiting, illustrating that many of these medical phobias are fuelled by misunderstandings and misinformation.

Myths and facts about medical phobias
Myth I: Fear of choking (pseudodysphagia): Sticking to soft foods will help you with a phobia of choking

Fact: This might seem like a practical solution to this problem, but if we avoid certain foods (otherwise known as an avoidance behaviour) we can actually reinforce the fear. If it's a vital food group, this could also leave you vulnerable to malnutrition. If our phobia relates to something niche, we can potentially sidestep it, but when it comes to something as important as eating it's always best to get to the root cause.

Myth 2: Fear of blood (hematophobia): Seeing blood should not cause fainting

Fact: Technically, this is true – it doesn't make evolutionary sense for us to faint when we're exposed to blood. But, as we know, when we're dealing with phobias we're not in the realm of rational thought. My clients *know* that they're experiencing a non-typical reaction, which is why they're seeking my help!

Myth 3: Fear of surgical operations or invasive medical procedures (tomophobia): Fear of surgery is just fear of pain

Fact: Surgery involves many more components than just potential pain – anaesthesia, fear of the unknown or losing your bodily autonomy, along with pain and potential complications. I remember one of my clients had huge anxiety about an upcoming surgery but didn't care about any of the above. With some exploration into the rest of her life, we worked out that it was the fear of being seen naked by someone she didn't know.

Myth 4: Fear of taking medication (pharmacophobia): It's just about the fear of side effects

Fact: Fear of taking medication can be related to fear of dependency, of the medication not working correctly, or it could be tied into a fear of choking. I've even met someone who had a phobic reaction to a very specific type of medication – a red capsule – related to a difficult childhood experience of having their stomach pumped after eating holly berries.

Myth 5: Fear of hospitals (nosocomephobia): It's just a fear of sickness

Fact: Hospitals can trigger a multitude of phobic reactions, from the environment and the smells to the sterile look. It could also be related to getting bad news, feeling humiliated or vulnerable, or the risk of an invasive procedure. Despite hospitals saving our lives and hopefully extending those of our loved ones, we also spend time in them while unwell and sometimes have to say goodbye to people there. As such, many people have had traumatic experiences related to hospitals.

Myth 6: Excessive online health-related searches (cyberchondria): More information will make you feel better
Fact: We've all been there; we have some sort of medical complaint, and rather than seeing a doctor we google our symptoms. And surprise, surprise! We get a range of different suggestions – your headache could be dehydration or you may be experiencing an aneurysm or brain cancer. As we talked about at the start of Part 2, too much information isn't always a good thing.

Myth 7: Fear of X-rays, MRI scans or radiation treatments (radiophobia): People with radiophobia are only afraid of the radiation
Fact: When we're going in for these treatments, especially MRI scans, we've often got some unanswered health questions, and waiting for the results can put us on edge. Also, they take place in very confined spaces, so it can co-occur with claustrophobia.

Myth 8: Fear of vomiting (emetophobia): People with emetophobia are just scared of feeling sick
Fact: No one enjoys being sick and there are myriad factors involved which can trigger phobias; we're out of control of our body, we might feel embarrassed, we might be scared of choking, and the sights and smells could repulse some people. We also rarely vomit when we are in good health, so the memory of doing so can be tied to a time when we were feeling terrible.

What are the dangers and causes of medical phobias?

As iatrophobia covers a broad range of more specific phobias, its causes can be just as wide ranging. Let's take a closer look at where some of those phobias might have come from.

▶ Medical phobias from a historical perspective ◀

Although records are sparse, it's likely that we've had some form of medical phobias since the dawn of humankind, even if we didn't quite understand what it was back then.

We're an inventive bunch, and as we've attempted to cure illnesses we've also come up with some fairly horrific ways to do so. Throughout our existence we've tried: bloodletting, trepanation (a hole being drilled into the skull), amputations carried out with nothing but brandy for an anaesthetic, intravenous milk infusions, smoking cigarettes (really) and sitting in cavities in decomposing whales.

I think we can all agree that being told that you were going to be subject to any of the above 'treatments' would be terrifying, even if you were absolutely sure it was going to cure you. It's not a stretch of the imagination to think this could have sowed the seeds for fear of doctors, medical procedures or medical settings.

We've also had our fair share of infectious diseases, from plagues in the Middle Ages to Ebola and malaria ravaging parts of the world even to this day. We've had multiple pandemics of respiratory infections like SARS, HINI and most recently COVID-I9. The public messaging encouraging us to wash our hands multiple times a day has also helped reinforce people's germ phobias, compounded compulsive sanitizing behaviours and avoidance of crowded places, and most likely nosophobia, the fear of contracting a chronic disease. The AIDS pandemic of the late twentieth century saw a rise in fear of contracting the disease, showing how contemporary events can shape medical phobias.

In the nineteenth century we advanced from pulling teeth in dentistry to filling cavities and doing root canals and the like. We also started doing routine extractions of teeth in some areas of the world, assuming that they would just rot. At the start, this was done without anaesthetic, which was incredibly painful and no doubt contributed to fear of dentists.

At the same time, we passed a medical milestone which has since saved millions of lives: mass vaccinations. Back then, it was the first time that most people had been injected with something, which could have contributed to needle phobia. In modern times, certain people have developed phobias of the actual vaccine rather than the delivery method due to some groups questioning their safety.

▶ Interconnected phobias ◀

As you'll have picked up, medical phobias are multifaceted and often overlap. Imagine the London Tube map – phobias move in the same way. They often intercept, overlap and connect to one another in the same way the lines do.

From the short, sharp pinch of a jab to the invasive nature of an endoscopy, many procedures involve a small level of pain. I'm sure that most of us can remember a time we weren't comfortable in a medical setting, which creates a natural overlap with algophobia, or fear of pain.

The fear of death (thanatophobia) also links to medical phobias. When we're in medical settings we often have to face our own mortality. Hospitals are often connected to memories of severe illnesses and life-threatening situations, so a fear of death can intensify the fear of doctors, hospitals or specific procedures. This might also then feed into a fear of developing a specific illness.

Social phobias also play a part in medical phobias; we are often in very vulnerable situations in front of medical professionals, which can be stressful. The stigma around mental health can also heighten fears of embarrassment; I remember a client worrying that her psychiatrist was going to think she was 'weird' for approaching her for help with her anxiety.

The fear of losing our control or autonomy can also factor into medical phobias; someone with tomophobia (fear of surgery) might be anxious they'll wake up from surgery paralyzed and from then on need help with day-to-day tasks. Or someone who has a tendency to faint might be worried that anything could happen to them when they were out.

Germophobia or mysophobia, a fear of germs or dirt, can also connect with medical phobias. Despite most medical environments being religiously cleaned, people may worry that they're hotbeds of contamination. Hospitals can be chaotic environments, which can also aggravate people's OCD or claustrophobia, especially if they need to be strapped to a stretcher. News stories covering events such as outbreaks of MRSA can also add fuel to this fire.

QUICK RECAP:

▶ Medical phobias can present in various ways and are as diverse as the field of medicine itself.

▶ Phobias can be triggered by a range of elements related to medical scenarios, from needles to germs to choking.

▶ Medical phobias often stem from specific triggers and past traumas, not just fear of pain or illness.

▶ Contemporary events, such as pandemics or disease outbreaks, can shape or reinforce certain medical phobias.

ENVIRONMENTAL PHOBIAS

For many, the natural world is a source of joy and serenity. The gentle lapping of waves against the shore, the rustling of leaves in a forest or the panoramic view from a mountain peak can evoke feelings of peace and a profound connection to the earth. However, these very same settings can instil fear and dread in others. Environmental phobias encompass a broad spectrum of fears, including those related to weather events such as tornadoes and hurricanes, natural elements like water and darkness, and specific phenomena such as fire, loud noises and even the act of throwing snow.

Chionophobia, or the fear of snow, can transform a picturesque Christmas card scene into a source of terror. Anemophobia, the fear of wind, might cause distress on what others would consider a refreshingly breezy day. Seismophobia, the fear of earthquakes, can make the very ground beneath our feet seem treacherous and untrustworthy.

Among the most prevalent environmental phobias is the fear of water, which manifests in various forms: aquaphobia, the fear of water in general; thalassophobia, the fear of deep bodies of water; cymophobia, the fear of waves; and potamophobia, the fear of rivers or running water. Studies in the United States have found that as many as 64 per cent of adults harbour a fear of deep, open waters, and between 2 per cent and 3 per cent have a full-blown phobia. While these figures are reportedly higher in children, for many individuals this fear diminishes over time. This was certainly the case for me.

As children, on the weekends my friends and I used to go to the public swimming pool. Then one day, when I was about six years old, I suddenly refused to go in. My friends were splashing around, while I remained on the side putting my toes in but refusing to swim. My fear lasted about a year before I started to get over it and got back to enjoying swimming again.

As the years went on, I'd long forgot about this fear let alone given any thought as to its causes.

Until one day I was working with an aquaphobic client who was about my age. As we explored the root cause of his fear, he remembered a cartoon he had seen which had a shark come through a tunnel and get into a swimming pool. This cartoon was the trigger for his phobia.

As he was telling me about this, my mind regressed back to that six-year-old me, thinking swimming pools are scary. I realized I had seen that cartoon, or one with the same plot anyway.

I wonder if the cartoon creators realized that their show had created a fear of water in at least two children – and I expect there were many more like us.

Many celebrities grapple with environmental phobias. David Hasselhoff, star of nineties television show *Baywatch*, ironically harbours a fear of water. Similarly, legendary basketball player

Michael Jordan has a phobia of water after having to abandon his drowning friend who was in danger of pulling him under. Actor Jodie Whittaker is scared of fire, stating, 'It's about not feeling in control of your surroundings, and internally I'm thinking worst-case scenario.'

Myths and facts about environmental phobias

Myth 1: If you have fear of fire (pyrophobia), you must be afraid of all sources of heat

<u>Fact</u>: Believe it or not, I've worked with a chef who had pyrophobia, even though he was always surrounded by red-hot ovens, gas burners, deep fat fryers and grills. However, if you were cruel enough to put him next to a bonfire he'd be a nervous wreck; his fear was specific to uncontrolled fire and originated when he saw his family's garage burn down.

Myth 2: Fear of tornadoes and hurricanes (lilapsophobia) makes sense because they're so dangerous

<u>Fact</u>: Even though the real danger isn't the real issue, sometimes it does help to know how unlikely it is. In our modern age, we'll usually get advance warnings to clear an area before a hurricane, and the odds of dying in a tornado is 1 in 5,693,092. However, it's worth remembering that you might never have seen such extreme weather and feeling afraid is natural.

Myth 3: Fear of rain (ombrophobia) is just a dislike of getting wet

<u>Fact</u>: It's not always the direct environmental aspect itself that we fear. You might absolutely love swimming but still be afraid of the rain; the sensory experience of it, the sound, the gloominess or people's attitudes.

Myth 4: People with fear of lightning and thunder (astraphobia) must also be afraid of loud noises

Fact: Phobias are always more complex than this. People might actually have no issue with the noise of the thunder but fear the unpredictability and perceived threat of thunderstorms.

Myth 5: Only children can have fear of the dark (nyctophobia)

Fact: While it is common for young children to be scared of the dark, it's not limited to them. I once had a middle-aged male client who had lived with the fear of darkness since his childhood. His fear was so strong that during the night he'd have multiple lights on in rooms he wasn't even trying to sleep in.

Myth 6: Fear of ferns (pteridophobia) is the same as fear of plants (botanophobia)

Fact: Pteridophobia is a specific subset of botanophobia. You might be able to enjoy the sight of blooming roses, the touch of daisy petals or the unique smell of lilacs but be sent into a panic attack at even the thought of a fern, let alone touching one. While this might seem innocuous to most, imagine panicking every time you walked past a green area where you might see a fern – that's pretty serious in my book.

Myth 7: Fear of snow (chionophobia) only affects people living in colder climates

Fact: You don't have to live in a cold climate to be afraid of snow. While it's true that it makes such fears more likely due to increased exposure, phobias don't pay attention to geographical boundaries.

In fact, coming from a hot climate could be the *cause* for developing chionophobia, due to snow's unfamiliarity. People might be afraid of its blinding whiteness, the coldness, its squeaky crunch, accidentally slipping over or the grey sludge that happens days after a snowstorm as it starts to melt and mix with dirt.

Causes of environmental phobias

As we have seen, environmental phobias can affect people no matter where they live or what kinds of environment they are most commonly exposed to. But are there any clear causes for such phobias?

▶ Environmental phobias from a historical perspective ◀

Throughout our history, we've likely been experiencing phobias related to our environment. They might seem totally irrational now, but in the past they may have kept us alive. For example, we didn't always live in houses and we were regularly exposed to the dangers of the wilderness. During these times, fear of water, fire or storms could have protected us and helped us to carry on evolving.

Nature has inspired fear, awe and respect in humans, and we've always had a complicated relationship with it. Thunderstorms, for example, were perceived as divine wrath by many ancient civilizations, leading to deeply ingrained fears that persist to this day. I once had a client called Roisin who had a crippling fear of thunderstorms – even hearing something that sounded like a distant rumble was enough to send her into panic mode. Even though we rarely have extreme thunderstorms in the UK, just the sound of the weather report could spin her into a cycle of dread.

We did some work together and she let go of the fear. On her next holiday to Scotland, she experienced a storm without panic, the once menacing thunder now seeming distant and less threatening.

We've always experienced natural disasters, which could have imprinted fear onto our collective consciousness. Earthquakes, tsunamis and volcanic eruptions led to seismophobia, aquaphobia and pyrophobia, respectively. This hasn't become better recently, as our twenty-four-hour news culture allows us to see *every single* disaster as it's happening worldwide. Most of these events seem bizarre and random, which could contribute to the fear of nature's unpredictable wrath.

▶ Interconnected environmental phobias ◀

Think about a thunderstorm and the potentially interconnected phobias that make up this fear. The bright flashes could trigger astraphobia (fear of lightning), the crashing sounds could cause brontophobia (fear of thunder) and the heavy rainfall could lead to ombrophobia (fear of rain). Each part of the storm could trigger people with multiple phobias, all suffering from the broader environmental phobia of lilapsophobia (fear of tornadoes or hurricanes), for example.

A fear of large bodies of water (thalassophobia) might happen alongside the fear of wide, open spaces (agoraphobia), with the vast, unending expanse of the ocean triggering a fear of the water and the open space it represents. On the other hand, cleithrophobia (fear of being trapped) can happen alongside chionophobia as people might fear being stuck and unable to move in a snowstorm or avalanche.

The fear of water and fear of drowning are another duo that are closely linked. Both can stem from traumatic experiences involving near-drowning incidents and also couple with the fear of the unknown that lurks beneath the surface of the water. Thalassophobia can also tie into this, where the vastness of the ocean creates an overwhelming sense of dread.

Nyctophobia, the fear of darkness, is another common fear that also has links to a variety of environmental phobias. The darkness itself can be a source of fear, due to its association with the unknown or potential danger. This fear can be heightened in certain situations, such as being in a dark forest (dendrophobia) or being alone in the dark (monophobia). Sometimes, the fear of darkness can even be connected to a fear of certain nocturnal animals, such as bats (chiroptophobia).

QUICK RECAP:

▶ Some 64 per cent of adults harbour a fear of deep, open waters, and between 2 per cent and 3 per cent have a full-blown phobia.

▶ Environmental phobias are fears associated with natural elements of our surroundings, such as water, fire, storms, darkness or loud noises. These fears are often unavoidable and can significantly affect everyday life.

▶ Historically, these environmental phobias might have had survival advantages.

▶ Our continuous exposure to global disaster news can intensify environmental phobias, as it reminds us of nature's unpredictable wrath.

FEAR OF SUCCESS AND FAILURE

As someone who works with fears, I'm sure you can guess the most common question I get asked: 'So, what are you afraid of?' Now, my usual tongue-in-cheek response is, 'Nothing I'm absolutely perfect,' but being human, of course we all have moments of fear. Luckily enough, I have the tools to deal with whatever might show up, but that hasn't stopped my fears popping up throughout my life.

Most people are familiar with the more common phobias, such as spiders or flying. However, there are more subtle fears that can lurk beneath the surface, still hindering our lives but not manifesting as obviously as others. I absolutely love the work I do – it's my life calling. I had reached a level of success in which I had helped many people, but I couldn't seem to go any further. I wanted to grow more, but something was holding me back. So, I decided to practise what I preach and sat down to work on myself.

Two events surfaced: one from childhood, hearing that rich and successful people were probably bad, and another from my teenage years, when I didn't feel worthy (otherwise know as imposter syndrome). I was shocked to discover that these beliefs had been with me for years, and in all the work I had done, I had missed them. I guess they weren't obvious. After all, it didn't make me stand on a chair screaming or run for the hills. It was just a fear that would rear its head from time to time and put the brakes on. After working on these triggers, it seemed almost overnight that I was receiving opportunities I had never had before.

In this section, we're going to take a look at these more hidden fears: success and failure. At surface level, these seem paradoxical. We're told we need to be successful to be happy, and most of us aspire to this. However, we can also shy away from success, thinking that it might cause stress, anxiety and increased demands and expectations, so we ultimately hold ourselves back from our true potential.

The same can be said for failure; I've met highly competent people whose fear held them back from pursuing their dreams. I've talked with clients who are so terrified that they'll disappoint their parents or partner by trying and not succeeding the first time that they're locked in paralysis. This fear keeps us in our comfort zone and stops us from taking the risks we need to take to grow as people.

Often, one of the unifying factors between these two fears is imposter syndrome. We doubt ourselves, our abilities, our intelligence and how much we deserve success. It also makes us balk at the thought of rising to the top of something – after all, the better we are, the more scrutiny we're under. Once we're doing well, we're constantly terrified the veil will slip and people will realize we got to our position through chance, so we downplay any achievements and never internalize our accomplishments.

I often see traits of perfectionism in my clients who come to me with fear of both success and failure, as it allows us to create impossibly high standards with huge consequences for not meeting them. Think for a second – can you imagine *anything* that's truly perfect? A perfect holiday? A perfect afternoon? A perfect car? Chances are, there's always some way you could think of improving anything, so applying this logic to our careers or personal lives puts us under an insurmountable pressure. If we're afraid of success, we might self-sabotage because we know that performing well tomorrow means we have to do even better the next day, resulting in an ever-increasing cycle of stress. On the other hand, if failure scares us, we might just throw our hands up in apathy at this seemingly impossible task.

Plenty of famous people have been affected by this too: Steve Jobs famously took eight years to buy a sofa; Lance Armstrong was so scared of losing that he turned to performance-enhancing drugs; and world-famous sculptor Michelangelo allegedly personally smashed pieces off one of his most famous statues, enraged at the imperfections in the marble.

Fear of success (achievemephobia)

In all my years practising, I've found that fear of success is far more common than we might think. I've spoken to CEOs, politicians and high-performing athletes who all suffer with this. Externally, it seems like they've made it, but internally their self-esteem and self-worth is so low that they're constantly in a state of heightened anxiety, terrified that one day people are going to realize they don't deserve all they've earned.

I've seen amazing feats of self-sabotage – recommending other, less competent employees for promotion over themselves, turning down offers of prominent art exhibits or just simply not showing up to work. Success doesn't just relate to the workplace, though – we can fear it in our personal lives too.

I remember one of my clients who had struggled with finding a meaningful relationship for years. Benjamin was a sensitive person who tended to internalize his issues, and throughout his life he had multiple turbulent relationships that ended badly. After experiencing the pain and heartache of each of these, he found himself putting his guard up more and more, scared to be involved romantically with anyone.

Eventually, he met a man who seemed different to his former partners; emotionally attuned and faithful, with whom he had loads of common interests. But when things started going well it also began to go wrong – he began questioning whether he *actually* deserved the happiness he was getting out of this relationship. Surely, if he's this content now, the *inevitable* break-up will be equally as heart-wrenching.

So, instead of fully committing to the relationship, he began to pull back and sabotage it. One day, to save himself the hurt and the pain, he abruptly ended things. When he arrived in my office, he was completely broken – he missed his former partner and had no idea why he had called it off. His fear had stopped him experiencing true love and happiness.

I've also encountered people for whom their position *is* their identity. They're worried that if their social circle sees them suddenly outperforming the rest of the group, they'll lose their sense of self and be ostracized from their friendship circle. They're immensely capable but worried that people will suddenly think they're arrogant. The reality is, if you're not aloof and rude in the place you're at now, you probably won't change with success. People are also misinformed about how this rise works – we're always fed media stories of 'overnight success', which is usually a marketing ploy. In reality, to do well at anything requires years of hard work and determination.

Fear of failure (atychiphobia)

On paper, it might seem like fear of failure could be a great thing. After all, surely this would just spur us on to be the very best version of ourselves, right? However, the truth is much more convoluted. Fear of failure can prevent us from even trying in the first place, and it can stand in the way of us recognizing when things have actually gone well. Often, the people I speak to have actually achieved what they set out to do, but not as they imagined it.

People with fear of failure often set impossible parameters to their goals – extremely difficult tasks completed the first time, in record time. They might see every past relationship as a complete waste of time, despite spending many happy years with each other and with hindsight growing emotionally.

That's not to say that every client of mine with fear of failure ends up achieving their goals – quite the opposite. Sometimes, people get too caught up visualizing arrays of disastrous outcomes to even begin the task. It's a deep-seated fear, often coming from difficult early life experiences, overly critical parents or cultural elements.

Myths about fear of success and failure

Myth I: You're probably just insecure if you're afraid of success

Fact: Phobias can be compartmentalized; while we can be incredibly confident in our professional abilities, we might doubt our ability to ever have a successful friendship or romantic relationship.

Myth 2: Fear of failure is always bad

Fact: A moderate degree of fear can be a driving force, motivating us to plan effectively, work hard and avoid unnecessary risks. There's nothing wrong with being cautious – it's the paralyzing fear of failure that can be harmful and hold us back.

Myth 3: Once you're successful, the fear of it goes away

Fact: People can often push through their fears and exist in a state of constant heightened anxiety – just because someone is afraid of success it doesn't mean they're not achieving it. We might do really well and hit a huge career milestone, but be absolutely dreading the next one.

Myth 4: Only lazy people fear success

Fact: I worked with a pianist who had spent tens of thousands of hours practising her instrument and was starting to become recognized for her skill. She was offered amazingly well-paid tours but couldn't bring herself to do them. For her, it wasn't the fact she lacked motivation, it was the thought of being on stage and being judged by thousands of people.

Myth 5: You can't be afraid of success and failure at the same time

Fact: Let me remind you of black-and-white thinking, also known as an all-or-nothing mindset. Let's say we're training for a marathon. Would it be reasonable to expect to be able to do 10km the first time you put your running shoes on? Chances are, you wouldn't. However, someone with black-and-white thinking might run as far as 9km on their first run and think it a complete disaster, further fuelling their phobia of failure. On the other hand, the fear of failure and knowing something is an impossible task might mean they consider even attempting it a catastrophic failure from the get-go, fostering a self-defeating cycle of avoidance and fear.

Myth 6: Fear of success or failure is inborn and unchangeable

Fact: Your fears are not immutable. They can change over time and with exposure to new experiences and perspectives.

Myth 7: Fear of success means you're a procrastinator

<u>Fact</u>: Procrastination can be a symptom, yes, but it's not a one-size-fits-all T-shirt. Many who fear success are in fact highly productive; they may simply fear the result of their efforts rather than the effort itself. You can love running the race but feel a bit winded at the thought of standing on the winners' podium.

Myth 8: Fear of failure is a sign you're not meant for the task

<u>Fact</u>: Here's a secret: even the most skilled acrobat can fear falling. Despite the fact that your brain might tell you otherwise, fear of failure doesn't mean you're unsuited for the task. It simply means you're overly concerned with the outcome.

Myth 9: Only people in high-pressure environments fear success

<u>Fact</u>: Fear of success isn't exclusive to elite banking, politics or sports. From artists to teachers to homemakers, anyone can experience this fear. It's not about the external environment as much as it is about internal perceptions and feelings.

Causes of fear of success and failure

The anxiety surrounding success and failure is perhaps familiar to many of us and it may be helpful to know more about where these fears have come from so we can begin to move on.

▶ Fear of success and failure from a historical perspective ◀

Throughout our history, plenty of historical stories could contribute to us fearing success or failure.

The father of modern genetics, Gregor Mendel, had his work on heredity in pea plants go mostly unnoticed while he was alive. Upset at his lack of recognition, he didn't even publish his later work on bees. Poet Emily Dickinson was also well known for being reclusive, and despite writing nearly 1,800 poems was too scared of rejection and failure to have them published – even the ones that were heavily edited. It took them being printed posthumously for her to get the recognition she deserved.

In more modern times, and especially with the advent of the internet and 'grind culture', we're forever being told that we're not working hard enough. We can't open social media without seeing someone with a bigger house than us, or a faster car or more money. This could spur people with fear of failure to use these 0.1 per cent of the population as a benchmark of what true success looks like, and not even try.

▶ Interconnected fears ◀

Fear of failure often co-occurs with sociophobia, which is the fear of social rejection. When we're scared of failing, we are often scared of how others will see us and possibly ridicule or judge us. This societal pressure can create a fear of even attempting to succeed, known as ergophobia.

I've worked with a client whose underlying fear wasn't success but death. He had watched his workaholic father die early through heart disease and equated success to early death and heartbreak for the rest of the family.

People with phonophobia, the fear of receiving a call or message, might also be afraid of success. We're all familiar with the high-flying business executive with a phone glued to their ear, getting contacted at all times of day – for some people, this is a nightmare.

Fear of success can also intertwine with hypengyophobia, which is the fear of responsibility. They see the rise up the corporate ladder or the idea of committing in a relationship and recognize the increase in responsibilities these things represent. Many of us would be proud to have such successes offered to us, but for someone with this condition they may see it as a loss of freedom.

Let's circle back to the beginning of this chapter. It's a common truth that most of us have some kind of fear, even if it doesn't readily show. When someone insists they are fearless, challenge them with a simple question: 'Is there a goal you've set that you're not meeting?' More often than not, if their goal is attainable yet remains out of reach, it's probable that they are being held back by a fear of success or failure.

QUICK RECAP:

▶ Fears of success and failure can be just as impactful as more commonly acknowledged phobias.

▶ Perfectionism is a trait regularly seen in people who fear success and failure, and it can lead to stress and potentially to self-sabotage.

▶ Fear of failure can lead us to avoid trying new things and to set unrealistic expectations, which can stand in the way of recognizing actual achievements.

▶ Fear of success isn't exclusive to high-pressure environments; anyone, irrespective of profession, can experience this fear.

FEAR OF FEAR

In every aspect of our lives, phobias can slip in and take a leading role – we've already covered many of the more well-known ones. However, one we've not talked about so far is the fear of fear itself. Fear of fear, or anxiophobia, is where we worry about experiencing a fear-inducing event in the future which puts us into a cycle of avoidance and further anxiety. This is called anticipatory anxiety, which isn't a standalone mental-health condition on its own but frequently happens alongside conditions like generalized anxiety disorder and panic disorder.

A client called Supreet came to me with a usual and unusual problem – they had won a prize at work. While most people would be elated at this, they were totally crestfallen as it meant getting up on stage and speaking in front of a crowd. Even thinking about it made their heart race, palms sweat and stomach turn with anticipation, even knowing they had months to prepare.

It wasn't that they didn't know *what* to say – they had time to script it. It wasn't that public speaking was an insurmountable phobia for them, as usually they could push through the nervousness. They were more worried that the symptoms of fear would be visible and they'd look 'stupid' in front of their colleagues. They were looking into an imaginary future and seeing themselves stumble over words, their hands shaking or their breathing becoming shallow and rapid. The anticipation of becoming nervous had become the fear itself, creating a feedback loop with seemingly no end.

It's not just fear of talking publicly that can tie into fear of fears and phobias. We might be afraid that we'll lose control as the adrenaline pumps through our body and we'll either overreact or totally freeze. Social norms dictate that we should act in a certain way, and we're always applauded for being calm under pressure. However, for those with a fear of fear it's not just a pressure – it feels like an immovable object.

Despite seeming outgoing and ever-confident, celebrities aren't immune to this. Actor Amanda Seyfried has talked about her anxiety, saying, 'I'll start worrying about my parents or my dog, and I'll picture him opening the window of my apartment and falling out, even though I can't get that thing open myself.' Likewise, fellow actor Ryan Reynolds has said, 'I have anxiety. I've always had anxiety, both in the lighthearted, "I'm anxious about this" kind of thing, and I've been to the depths of the darker end of the spectrum, which is not fun.'

Myths about fear of fear
Myth I: If you experience fear of fear, you're losing your sanity
Fact: Fear is an emotionally charged response, and when it becomes recursive it can certainly feel overwhelming, even unhinging, but this doesn't mean you're losing your sanity. Feelings of extreme dread are symptoms of anxiety, but they don't mean that your mental state is deteriorating.

Myth 2: Fear of fear is physically dangerous

Fact: Panic attacks can make us feel like we are about to die as our mouth goes dry, we get dizzy and our heart races. Often, people's biggest fear is that they're going to have – or are having – a heart attack. The good news is that panic attacks *don't* cause heart attacks, and our body's response to fear is a survival mechanism, a primal 'fight or flight' reaction that isn't designed to harm us but to protect us. However, being constantly under stress has been linked to a number of health conditions, so it's worth doing the work to let it go.

Myth 3: Fear of fear will always lead to a full-blown panic attack

Fact: While fear of fear can lead to heightened anxiety, it doesn't always culminate in a panic attack. Think of it like a pot of water on the stove – just because it's heating up doesn't mean it's going to boil. Even when it does, the heat might only cause gentle ripples rather than a full, rolling boil. In the same way, the escalation of fear can vary – it could cause mild distress, moderate discomfort or in some instances a more severe reaction like a panic attack.

Myth 4: It's incredibly rare to have a fear of fear

Fact: Anxiety disorder, which is often the main culprit behind fear of fear, is incredibly common. It's thought that around 4.05 per cent of the global population have some form of this, which equates to hundreds of millions of people.

Myth 5: Fear of fear means you can't handle stress

Fact: Many people with high anxiety sensitivity are often able to manage high-pressure situations successfully. It's the specific cycle of fearing the sensation of fear that becomes an issue.

Myth 6: Fear of fear means you can't deal with embarrassment

Fact: Fear of fear can involve a fear of embarrassment, but it isn't about people's inability to handle embarrassment. It's more centred on a dread of the anxiety they associate with potentially embarrassing situations.

Myth 7: Tackling a specific phobia doesn't require addressing anticipatory anxiety

Fact: Anticipatory anxiety typically reinforces a phobia, making it more entrenched. It's often more effective to address the anticipatory anxiety first, because the dread of a feared event can create strong resistance to facing the phobia and can involve secondary gain. By dealing with the anticipatory anxiety, you reduce the hold the phobia has and may find it easier to confront and overcome the specific fear afterwards.

Causes and dangers of fear of fear

Fear of fear itself is perhaps one of the most understandable phobias in this book – why would we not be afraid of feeling afraid? – but let's look a little deeper into where this anxiety might have stemmed from.

▶ Fear of fear from a historical perspective ◀

During humans' earlier, more tribal existence, our fear was largely focused on threats to our lives like famine, natural disasters and being attacked by rival tribes or vicious predators. This is how our fear response evolved, but as we have become more complex, so has our relationship with fear.

In the Middle Ages, we had fears that were tied to our religious beliefs and we believed in sin, divine punishment and being sentenced to burning in hell if we did something perceived as wrong. Much of this was largely out of our control, and no doubt many people existed in perpetual states of being afraid.

There was a huge cultural shift in the eighteenth century as we began to think of fear (and the rest of our emotions) as natural rather than spiritually driven. As religious fears started to die down, we became more concerned with societal and personal issues, which may have sowed the seeds for fear of social interactions.

The two world wars in the first half of the twentieth century showed the world new sources of fear and anxiety, and PTSD (initially known as shell shock) became part of the wider public discourse. The fact that it wasn't understood left soldiers terrified of the fear they might experience when they were sent to battle.

The invention of the internet hasn't helped matters and has given rise to a new kind of fear. We now never know if we're going to open our phone to news of a new war, a pandemic or an act of terror.

QUICK RECAP:

▷ Anxiophobia is the fear of fear and affects about 4 per cent of the population.

▷ It often pairs with a cycle of avoidance, known as anticipatory anxiety, and is commonly associated with generalized anxiety disorder and panic disorder.

▷ Fear of embarrassment or failure in anticipated situations can fuel the cycle of fear, leading to continued dread and avoidance.

▷ Concerns about losing control from adrenaline surges and the desire to adhere to social expectations can intensify anxiophobia.

ODD AND UNUSUAL PHOBIAS

Everyone has experienced some sort of fear at some point in their life, and a lot of phobias are widely known about. People don't usually question fears of heights or spiders, but there are other less common fears that people might see as strange or even ridiculous, such as phobias of beards, not being with a mobile phone or peanut butter sticking to the roof of their mouth. I was absolutely disgusted recently when a TV presenter was goading people for being scared of balloons or clowns. These fears might be more niche, but they are just as debilitating as any other phobias and have the capacity to put people into a state of complete terror. Most of the time, they have their roots in other phobias, such as the peanut butter example being tied to a fear of choking.

The press contacted me to work with a woman called Hannah, who had a very unique phobia – the fear of tinsel. This might seem quaint to some people, but for Hannah it had serious consequences. Most of us look forward to Christmas – it's a special time of year when we can be with our loved ones, exchange gifts

273

and be merry. But for Hannah, it was a looming spectre on the horizon throughout the year.

Even the thought of seeing tinsel was enough to make her feel sick. Her aversion caused her to spend five Christmases alone. She wasn't able to attend work events, and going out during the festive period was a nightmare for her.

On working with her we found the root cause: a seemingly innocent childhood incident when her cousins wrapped her in tinsel. The scratchy texture and feelings of helplessness and being trapped caused a very strong reaction and for her fear of those emotions to continue into adulthood. Although what's on the surface may seem odd or even funny to some people, when you dig down it can make perfect sense. After our session, Hannah was able to enjoy Christmas again.

Celebrities with unusual phobias

1. Johnny Depp had this to say about clowns: 'Something about the painted face, the fake smile. There always seemed to be a darkness lurking just under the surface, a potential for real evil.'

2. Kendall Jenner has trypophobia (fear of holes), writing on her blog: 'Things that could set me off are pancakes, honeycomb or lotus heads (the worst!). It sounds ridiculous but so many people actually have it!'

3. Oprah Winfrey has chiclephobia, or fear of gum, stating, 'My grandmother used to save it in little rows in the cabinet. I'd be scared to touch it because it was so gross, so I have a thing about gum.'

4. Matthew McConaughey is frightened of revolving doors, saying, 'I worry they'll cut me in half. Strangers will see me tense up and hold my hand as I'm going through them. I'm

constantly worried that I'm not going to make it through the door alive.'

5. Pamela Anderson has a fear of mirrors, or eisoptrophobia.

6. Billy Bob Thornton is scared of both bright colours and vintage furniture.

7. Christina Ricci, famous for her role in *The Addams Family*, suffers from botanophobia, or fear of plants, saying, 'If I have to touch one, after already being repulsed by the fact that there is a plant indoors, then it just freaks me out.'

8. David Beckham has a fear of disorder, known as ataxophobia. He's said that he has a compulsion to organize everything in a straight line or in pairs.

9. Megan Fox has papyrophobia, or fear of paper, revealing that she has to keep a cup of water next to her if she's reading a book.

More unusual phobias

Fear of being without a mobile phone (nomophobia): This is certainly a phobia for our more modern times! It creates anxiety when we don't have connectivity or charge, which is no doubt exacerbated by how dependent on them many of us now are. This can result in physical symptoms like headaches, as well as more severe mental issues, such as depression and isolation.

Apart from feeling stressed and overwhelmed when away from a device, nomophobes also experience irrational thoughts where they may be convinced that something bad will happen if they are not reachable through their mobile phones at all times.

In extreme cases, nomophobia can lead to an addiction disorder where people become so reliant on technology that it interferes with daily life and activities outside of work or school.

Fear of bathing (ablutophobia): Ablutophobia is an extreme and irrational fear of bathing, washing yourself or cleaning.

This phobia may be linked to past experiences, such as feeling suffocated while underwater or being sprayed with cold water. It can also occur due to a traumatic event in the home during childhood which promotes strong negative associations surrounding the activity of bathing.

Fear of beards (pogonophobia): Beards, moustaches, goatees – all are personal expressions that can shape the way we look and carry ourselves in public.

However, for some people the sight of a beard may be met with fear and anxiety, due to a condition known as pogonophobia.

The causes of pogonophobia range from past experiences with bearded individuals (such as bullying) that leave negative associations, to misplaced stigmatization towards certain cultures (e.g. associating bearded muslims with terrorism), to self-insecurities regarding people's own ability/inability to grow beards.

Fear of cheese (turophobia): Turophobia causes an overwhelming fear of cheese and dairy products. This anxiety-inducing disorder has been known to impact people in many ways, causing sensory overload by the smell, taste or texture of cheese.

People with turophobia can also be triggered by certain forms of cheese, such as melted cheese or cheesecake. This might seem like a more light-hearted phobia, but in rare cases this fear can be so extreme that it even impacts social activities or where they choose to shop.

One potential cause is an aversion to its taste, which may develop if someone overindulged in cheese and subsequently felt ill during their youth. Another possibility is a negative reaction to the aroma of cheese. Those with a heightened sensitivity may have had a particularly bad experience as a child, associating the smell of cheese with unpleasant feelings. Choking on cheese can also instil a lasting fear.

Fear of the colour yellow (xanthophobia): People with xanthophobia experience immense anxiety when confronted with yellow objects, such as clothing items, an artwork featuring the colour or even something as small and seemingly insignificant as a post-it note.

The fear often has distinctly negative origins – unhappy experiences associated with the colour yellow are thought to be one of the primary triggers for developing this phobia.

Those affected might express a strong aversion toward any form of yellow, avoiding items such as stationery products made in bright hues or refusing to participate in activities taking place in rooms full of mustard walls out of utter terror.

Fear of long words (hippopotomonstrosesquipedaliophobia): This phobia might appear as a cruel irony. It is frequently associated with previous embarrassing experiences or difficulties in reading, and it can also be related to fears of public speaking and social judgement. This fear tends to be most prevalent in environments like academia, where complex language is often used.

Fear of buttons (koumpounophobia): Koumpounophobia is a word derived from Latin and Greek language roots. While some people may experience intense fear when thinking about or seeing buttons, others may instead feel extreme disgust towards them.

Fear of birthday celebrations (fragapanophobia): People with this phobia may dread the social expectations, noise or other specific aspects of celebrations, such as balloons or fireworks, often causing people to avoid these occasions altogether. It can also take a more personal note, with people fearing aging and the expectations that we place on our achievements.

Fear of Christmas (Christougenniatikophobia): This can come from a wide range of factors, including trauma, social anxieties, tinsel (as we mentioned earlier), the thought of someone entering your house without permission or an aversion to Christian symbols. It can tie into the festive lifestyle, which usually includes increased drinking, stress including over money and seeing family, and overeating, also bringing up feelings of comparison, loss and dissatisfaction.

Fear of Halloween (Samhainophobia): This shouldn't be a surprising one – it's a festive season dedicated entirely to spooky, scary things! However, this phobia can turn this playful occasion into a time of significant dread and distress, often due to fear of darkness, fear of ghosts or supernatural entities, fear of masks and costumes, fear of death symbolism and of course fear of bugs – even if they are plastic.

Fear of throwing things away (disposophobia): People with this condition usually hold onto objects that seemingly have little or no value, hoarding them because they feel overwhelmed with anxiety at the prospect of parting with them and often feeling that the objects have sentimental value or could possibly be useful in the future. Once just thought of as laziness, we now understand that this is a manifestation of a fear of loss, connecting physical possessions to emotional attachments.

Fear of clowns (coulrophobia): The fear of clowns can be traced back to a variety of factors. One possible cause is the uncanny appearance of clowns, with their exaggerated makeup, brightly coloured costumes and oversized features. This exaggerated and distorted appearance can be unsettling to some individuals, triggering a sense of unease and apprehension. Furthermore, the fear of clowns may stem from negative associations or traumatic experiences. Media portrayals of evil clowns, such as in horror movies or literature, have contributed to the popularization of the fear. Additionally, personal encounters with them during childhood, such as a distressing or uncomfortable experience at a circus or birthday party, can leave a lasting impact on an individual's perception of clowns.

These examples illustrate the diversity and complexity of phobias, though there are many more, hopefully showing you that almost anything can become a source of intense fear for some people – and that it's not something to hide from or be embarrassed by.

IT'S TIME TO FACE YOUR FEAR

As you reach the end of this section, you've explored the science of phobias. You've navigated through the seven steps and learned how to confront them and examine your phobia from all perspectives. You've gained understanding about how phobias form and the myriad forms they can take. So, what's left? Well, the moment has come to face your fear.

At the outset of this book, I highlighted the potential pitfalls of confronting a phobia unprepared. Premature exposure therapy can, at best, result in slow progress and substantial stress, and at worst it can trigger re-traumatization. However, once you've taken the necessary steps to reduce and remove your fear, a critical stage arrives: the moment of reality when the only way to truly know your progress is by testing it.

If thinking about facing your fear still fills you with apprehension, it might indicate that some exercises require revisiting. There might be unresolved aspects that you need to address, or you might need to re-read about your specific phobia again in detail. However, if you feel ready to confront your fear and there's a growing sense of readiness within you, a key question emerges: how do you go about it? What's the most effective strategy to ensure a sense of achievement?

What steps can you take to make it manageable?

Now, there are people who don't do things by half. I had one client mortified of flying who had volunteered for a skydiving jump. They went from zero to 100 in tackling their fear. Another individual, petrified of ascending beyond three floors in a skyscraper, opted to confront their fear by scaling the tallest building they could find. These cases are not too dissimilar to the pitches I have had from several TV companies that want to adopt a dramatic method to show people's fears.

Of course, if you have taken on big challenges a small one might seem easy by comparison. However, unless you're still in all-or-nothing thinking, for most people a gradual approach is probably more beneficial.

The key is to step beyond your comfort zone gradually. Growth doesn't happen when you are staying in the familiar and not stretching yourself, yet it's important not to push so far as to trigger overwhelming feelings. Therefore, breaking it down into manageable steps is useful.

▶ Think about your specific phobia and identify the least intimidating challenge you could face. If you're afraid of spiders, could you tolerate the presence of a money spider or even a cartoon picture of one? What might the next incremental challenge be?

▶ The same approach applies to duration. For someone with a fear of public speaking, the initial challenge might involve addressing a small group for five minutes. The next step could then be addressing a slightly larger group for a longer duration. For agoraphobia you could start with going out on your front porch for few minutes, then progressing to walking down the block, then visiting a small park and so on.

▶ Now take the time to list out all the incremental steps you could take to challenge yourself and help you grow.

▶ Then it's just about taking action without procrastination and implementing the steps you've outlined.

▶ Monitor your feelings as you do each step. If it feels easy speed up the process, and if it feels difficult slow it down a bit. You can also practise the processes you have learned and anchor any of your successes. However, if the emotion is more like relief don't anchor it: you'd just be anchoring tension.

CONCLUSION

Congratulations on making it to this point in the book and being willing to do everything you can to face your fear.

What we have covered in this book and the tips contained within it should have you feeling ready to take on the world with confidence.

Since overcoming my fear of flying, I've travelled the world, seen sights I could never have visited, enjoyed vacations in new places and met people that were off-limits to me.

I've seen thousands of clients for whom similar opportunities opened up once they had changed their phobia. There is, however, one thing that can be missed when you are caught up in your fears and phobias, and it's that overcoming a fear is not just about you.

As I talked about earlier in this book, the moment I was laughed at in school I decided that I was never going to speak in public again. But on working with the processes that I have shared with you, I was able to change all that.

There was one memorable moment that really shifted my perceptions about my fear of speaking. I was taking a course where I had to get on stage and speak. It was scary and I made a lot of mistakes.

My mentor took me to one side and looked me straight in the eyes.

'You know what, Chris?' he said. 'You are being really selfish.'

At first, I was a little shocked, and then I felt angry. 'Selfish?' I asked, glaring at him.

'Yes, selfish,' he replied

Now my blood was boiling. I got defensive and started trying to explain how I was feeling.

But then he said something that has stuck with me ever since.

He said, 'Well, when you're on stage, you're only thinking about yourself. You're worrying that you'll make a mistake or what other people think of you.'

He carried on, 'But when you can stop thinking about yourself and instead look outwards to what you can give to your audience; when you pay attention to what they need to learn, how you can help them and make them feel, then you will be free from your fear.'

He added as he walked away: 'You know, Chris, when you think about the audience and not yourself, it's very hard to be fearful.

He was right. Since I overcame my fear of speaking, I have presented to many groups and not just on stage but also speaking to camera. I have reached so many more people. I often get contacted by people just to be told how much I have made a difference to their lives.

So even if you are not motivated to let go of your phobia for yourself, then what about others? What is the difference you can make to your family, friends, children and more?

And like so many other people have discovered, you'll never know the difference you can make to yourself and the world until you let go of your phobias and face your fears.

ABOUT THE AUTHOR

Christopher Paul Jones, is a speaker, author, coach and therapist. His work has been featured regularly on international TV, radio and in the press, including the BBC, Channel 4, Canada's CBC, *Hello*, *GQ*, *Harper's Bazaar*, *Marie Claire* and national newspapers. Christopher's clients come from all over the world to see him in his consulting rooms on London's world-renowned Harley Street, and have included Hollywood actors and Oscar nominees, models, musicians, presenters, and celebrities.

Never one to follow the status quo, Christopher pioneered an integrated approach combining mainstream psychology with cutting edge techniques to develop the Integrated Change System. Christopher is passionate about pulling people out of their negative patterns of behaviour and showing them how to be free of the emotions that trap them like mental quicksand. His high-energy, fast-paced coaching approach strikes a delicate balance between laser-focused, unconventional, and light-hearted to create change swiftly at an incredibly deep level, ridding his clients of phobias, fears, and anxiety at lightning speed.

When he's not fixing clients, Christopher and his family can be found living their vision of freedom in London and exploring the surrounding countryside with their equally inspired dog.

You can find out more at www.christopherpauljones.com

READER RESOURCES

To help you implement the strategies in this book, I've shared a range of tools.

Scan the QR code here:

GLOSSARY: 101 PHOBIAS

Ablutophobia: Fear of bathing, washing or cleaning

Acrophobia: Fear of heights

Aerophobia: Fear of flying

Agoraphobia: Fear of open or crowded spaces

Aichmophobia: Fear of pointed objects like needles

Ailurophobia: Fear of cats

Algophobia: Fear of pain

Arachnophobia: Fear of spiders

Astraphobia: Fear of thunder and lightning

Atelophobia: Fear of imperfection

Atychiphobia: Fear of failure

Autophobia: Fear of being alone

Barophobia: Fear of gravity

Bathmophobia: Fear of stairs or steep slopes

Belonephobia: Fear of pins and needles

Bibliophobia: Fear of books

Cacophobia: Fear of ugliness

Carcinophobia: Fear of cancer

Catoptrophobia: Fear of mirrors

Chiroptophobia: Fear of bats

Chronophobia: Fear of time

Claustrophobia: Fear of confined spaces

Coulrophobia: Fear of clowns

Cyberphobia: Fear of computers

Cynophobia: Fear of dogs

Decidophobia: Fear of making decisions

Dendrophobia: Fear of trees

Dentophobia: Fear of dentists

Domatophobia: Fear of houses or being in a house

Dromophobia: Fear of crossing streets

Dystychiphobia: Fear of accidents

Emetophobia: Fear of vomiting

Entomophobia: Fear of insects

Ephebiphobia: Fear of teenagers

Equinophobia: Fear of horses

Febriphobia: Fear of fever

Gamophobia: Fear of marriage

Gelotophobia: Fear of being laughed at

Genuphobia: Fear of knees

Glossophobia: Fear of speaking in public

Gnosiophobia: Fear of knowledge

Haphephobia: Fear of being touched

Heliophobia: Fear of the sun

Hemophobia: Fear of blood

Herpetophobia: Fear of reptiles

Hippopotomonstrosesquipedaliophobia: Fear of long words

Hoplophobia: Fear of firearms

Hydrophobia: Fear of water

Iatrophobia: Fear of doctors and medical care

Ichthyophobia: Fear of fish

Jactitationphobia: Fear that one is boasting

Katsaridaphobia: Fear of cockroaches

Lachanophobia: Fear of vegetables

Ligyrophobia: Fear of loud noises

Limnophobia: Fear of lakes

Megalophobia: Fear of large objects

Melissophobia: Fear of bees

Mysophobia: Fear of germs or dirt

Necrophobia: Fear of dead things

Noctiphobia: Fear of the night

Nomophobia: Fear of being without a mobile phone

Nosocomephobia: Fear of hospitals

Nyctophobia: Fear of darkness

Ombrophobia: Fear of rain

Optophobia: Fear of opening one's eyes

Ornithophobia: Fear of birds

Papyrophobia: Fear of paper

Pathophobia: Fear of disease

Phasmophobia: Fear of ghosts

Phobophobia: Fear of phobias

Photophobia: Fear of light

Potamophobia: Fear of rivers or running water

Pyrophobia: Fear of fire

Quadraphobia: Fear of the number four

Rhabdophobia: Fear of being severely criticized; also fear of magic

Samhainophobia: Fear of Halloween

Scelerophobia: Fear of criminals

Scolionophobia: Fear of school

Selenophobia: Fear of the moon

Sociophobia: Fear of social evaluation

Somniphobia: Fear of sleep

Tachophobia: Fear of speed

Taurophobia: Fear of bulls

Technophobia: Fear of technology

Thalassophobia: Fear of deep water

Thanatophobia: Fear of death

Thermophobia: Fear of heat

Tokophobia: Fear of pregnancy or childbirth

Tomophobia: Fear of surgical operations

Toxiphobia: Fear of poison

Traumatophobia: Fear of injury

Tremophobia: Fear of trembling

Trichopathophobia: Fear of hair

Triskaidekaphobia: Fear of the number 13

Turophobia: Fear of cheese

Urophobia: Fear of urine or urinating

Vehophobia: Fear of driving

Wiccaphobia: Fear of witches and witchcraft

Xanthophobia: Fear of the colour yellow

Ymophobia: Fear of contrariety

Zoophobia: Fear of animals